PRAISE FOR
SEASONS OF A WILD LIFE

Naber's work is a joyous, yet realistic ride through a year's seasons on her land. With a knowledgeable, intuitive, and environmentally attuned view into the relationships between humans and ecosystems, the author makes insightful suggestions for how to live more harmoniously with nature in this age of challenge and change. Providing cultural background for seasonal festivities, legends, and spirits, Naber stirs up the mythological unconscious latent in everyone, enriching our understanding of the ways we celebrate the passage of time. *Seasons of a Wild Life* is also a treasury of herbal remedies, naturalist observations, and ancestral wisdom beckoning the reader to slow down and marvel at nature's resilience.

JESSICA CAREW KRAFT   Author of *Why We Need to Be Wild*

What a great pleasure it is to read *Seasons of a Wild Life*—clear, agile and multi-dimensional writing, the capacity to live a life of exquisite tactile earthly contact and illuminating awareness, the blend of fact and information, point of view and creature orientation, inspiration and grounded dailiness, all work together to make this a great book.

Annette Naber weaves this effortlessly—so that the flow of seasons, with their distinct stories and yet integrated natures, come through these pages. The book overflows with timeless wisdom, LIFE speaking to us with a very beautiful, vivid voice. I can't recommend this book highly enough."

JOHN FOX   Founder, The Institute for Poetic Medicine, author of *Poetic Medicine* and *Finding What You Didn't Lose.*

Weaving poetry, plant-lore, myth, ritual, and hands-on experience of the land, Annette Naber crafts an irresistible invitation to reconnect with Nature—our own and the Earth's.

MARY REYNOLDS THOMPSON   Author of *Reclaiming the Wild Soul* and *The Way of the Wild Soul Woman*

I LOVE this book. A wonderful weaving of story and science and myth. In *Seasons of a Wild Life*, psychotherapist, naturalist, and forager Annette Naber encourages readers "to apprentice yourself to whatever environment you find yourself in." By sharing a year's worth of her own stewardship practices in the Virginia Highlands, Naber not only poetically recounts the daily lessons she learns from the native plants, insects, wildlife, and weather on her farm, but she also brings a global historical perspective on the deep human myths that still provide guiding principles and metaphors for living well in harmony with Nature. In the manner of Robin Wall Kimmerer's *Braiding Sweetgrass*, Naber offers us an accessible and deeply felt memoir and guide to experiencing nature that will change how you pay attention to the passing of a month and awaken your appreciation of the forces and rhythms of nature so often obscured by the frenetic pace of the digital world.

GEORGANN EUBANKS   Author of six books from the University of North Carolina Pres, including *Saving the Wild South: The Fight for Native Plants on the Brink of Extinction*.

I cannot overstate how well written, engaging, and moving each chapter is. From poem to myth and personal experience, I feel held by, and included in, the author's life and haunts.

MICHAEL WATSON, PHD   Blogger at *Dreaming the World*.

Seasons of a Wild Life is a thoughtful and charming anthology of nature poems, encounters with animals and plants, musings on myths across cultures, and thought-provoking questions that inspire us to a deeper examination of our lives. The author encompasses a wide range of topics, yet writes lightly, holding the reader's interest throughout the cycle of the year. I thoroughly enjoyed it." **MO WILDE**   Author of *The Wilderness Cure*

Annette Naber deftly weaves nature mythology from around the world into this inspiring gem of a book about seasonal changes on her Virginia farm. I savored every page of this remarkable book."

LAURA DAVIS   Author of *The Courage to Heal* and *The Burning Light of Two Stars*

As inspirational as it is informative, in *Seasons of a Wild Life*, Annette invites her readers to rediscover their connection with the natural world. She takes us on her journey from worldly-wise D.C. clinical psychologist to self-sufficient homesteader in the Virginia Highlands. Through poetry and evocative prose, she guides us through a calendar year on her farm offering a glimpse of the life many of us dream about. Each chapter focuses on one month, diving into the connection between the landscape, the ecosystem, and her experience, offering unique inner connections to related mythology and folktales, as well as gardening wisdom, self-sufficiency tips, and journaling prompts for personal reflection. Whether you're dreaming of finding your own homestead or needing to find a way to reconnect to nature where you are, get this book!

Read it one month at a time and travel through the year and the seasons with Annette's insights, or devour it whole. *Seasons of a Wild Life* is a beautiful call to reconnection with who we are in relationship to the planet we share.

What a wonderful book! I love it!

ANDREA M. SLOMINSKI, PHD
Author of *The Victory of Ariadne*

The more we move through the seasons of our lives with a poem in our hearts and a recounting of nature's forces, the more we walk whole upon the earth. That is what Annette Naber does as she takes us through the garden landscape of her wild life punctuated with myth, meaningful symbolism, animal and plant medicine, wild food foraging, and more. In *Seasons of a Wild Life*, she re-educates our thinking about how to connect with nature and how to embrace the challenges we face when pursuing our dreams—even those given to us by a future self. I am grateful to Annette for writing this book in answer to her question: How can we reclaim our lost connection to nature? This book is not to be read once but to be worked with perennially through each month and season of the year.

> **THEA SUMMER DEER, D.S.P.S.** Author of *Wisdom of the Plant Devas: Herbal Medicine for a New Earth*

In *Seasons of a Wild Life*, author Annette Naber invites us to ramble through the woods and meadows of her Virginia Highlands home, to meet her plant and animal neighbors and learn their ways. Gently and beautifully, Naber's wisdom, garnered through years of study and experience, unfolds before us, and we see our connections to the generous, wonder-filled world around us. As we turn the pages of this monthly almanac, we observe changes in the gardens and landscapes and become better acquainted with medicinals and food that can be foraged from the wild. We pay homage to the wisdom of ancient myths from around the world and to the animals who call this land home. Graced with poetry and personal stories, this is a book that you will want to savor slowly, month by month, year after year, as it draws you more fully into the seasons of your own wonderful wild life."

> **LEAH RAMPY** Author of *Earth & Soul: Reconnecting amid Climate Chaos* (2024); co-author with Beth Norcross of *Discovering the Spiritual Wisdom of Trees* (2025)

Clearly crafted with love and her life's experience, Annette has gifted us an exquisite and intimate journey through the seasons of the year. She has beautifully woven world mythology, plant, stone and earth medicine in with the tapestry of her personal wisdom and teachings as a lifelong devotee of Nature. More than anything, Annette captures the essence of learning through her story telling, humor and deep respect for this Great Green World we inhabit. An extraordinary way to learn about Nature in all her guises. From her years of kitchen/homestead wisdom to brilliantly researched lore, this is one book that you will want to revisit to accompany your days deepening your relationship with Nature.

> **KAT MAIER, RH (AHG)** Author of *Energetic Herbalism: A Guide to Sacred Plant Traditions Integrating Vitalism, Ayurveda and Chinese Medicine.*

What a rich and beautiful book about the natural world and the inner processes evoked by investing deep attention into our environment. While Naber made the shift to rural living later in life, she comes across as someone who has always been immersed in land and sky and animal habitat. As she writes about her demanding work in home and garden, she reminds us that homesteading is not the dreamy relationship with nature we might imagine, but a lived stewardship. The journaling prompts at the end of each chapter invite the reader into deeper relationship with their own experience of nature.

> **JOYCE KORNBLATT** Author of *Mother Tongue* (2022) and four other novels

Annette Naber has chosen a path many dream of but few have the courage to attempt: living simply on the land in respectful partnership with nature. Her extraordinary memoir invites us into an intimate daily dance with the wild that is breathtaking, awe-inspiring, or hair-raising—sometimes all at once. *Seasons of a Wild Life* guides us on a heroine's journey through a fascinating landscape populated by bears and bluebells, maples and mountain lions, nature gods and goddesses. It leaves us in awe of the wisdom and wonders of the wild, reconnected with rich traditions of reverence for nature, and inspires us to walk more gently on the Earth and honor our own true nature.

KAI SIEDENBURG   Author of the *Poems of Earth and Spirit* series

Seasons
of a
Wild Life

Seasons
of a
Wild Life

ANNETTE NABER, PH.D.

BOLD
STORY
PRESS

CHEVY CHASE, MD

Bold Story Press, Chevy Chase, MD 20815
www.boldstorypress.com

Disclaimer

The author does not provide medical advice or prescribe the use of any technique or herbal remedies for the treatment of physical, medical, or emotional symptoms. Please consult a qualified health professional for diagnostic and treatment purposes. Information presented here is merely for educational purposes. If readers choose to forage for wild plants, they are responsible for obtaining qualified advice for identifying and preparing such plants. The author and publisher assume no responsibility for your actions.

First edition: October 2024
Library of Congress Control Number: 2024921884
ISBN: 978-1-954805-78-1 (hardcover)
ISBN: 978-1-954805-68-2 (paperback)
ISBN: 978-1-954805-69-9 (e-book)

Cover and interior design by KP Books

Printed in the United States of America
10 9 8 7 6 5 4 3 2 1

CONTENTS

Introduction   1

JANUARY

Poem: Bare Bones   5
Incubation   5
Winter Deities & Frost Giants   7
Bear   8
January Garden & Landscape 10
Foraged Plant: Jerusalem Artichoke (*Helianthus tuberosus*) . . . 11
Mending & Repair 12
January Summary 16
Writing Prompts for Self-Reflection 17

FEBRUARY

Poem: Winter's Tail 19
Resilience 19
Brigid 20
Owl 22
February Garden & Landscape 24
Foraged Food: Maple Syrup 25
Avoiding Food Waste 26
February Summary 31
Journaling Prompts for Self-Reflection 32

MARCH

Poem: Morning Prayer 33
Resurrection of the Life Force 33
Frost Giants & Sun Gods 36
Coyote 37
March Garden & Landscape 39

Foraged Plant: Purple Dead Nettle (*Lamium purpureum*) 40
Spring Cleaning. 41
March Summary 43
Journaling Prompts for Self-Reflection 43

APRIL

Poem: Green 45
Fertility, New Growth & Viriditas. 45
Eostre & Ostara 47
Hare/Rabbit 49
April Garden & Landscape. 51
Foraged Plant: Common Chickweed (*Stellaria media*) 53
Foraging Wild Green Superfoods. 54
April Summary 59
Journaling Prompts for Self-Reflection 60

MAY

Poem: Full Moon 61
Exuberant Fertility, Sacred Marriage 62
Beltane & the Green Man 63
Hummingbird 66
May Garden & Landscape 68
Foraged Plant: Stinging Nettle (*Urtica dioica*) 69
Gardening as Therapy & Resistance 71
May Summary 73
Journaling Prompts for Self-Reflection 73

JUNE

Poem: Refuge in the Peace of Wild Things 75
Wildness & Domestication. 75
Flora & the Oak King, Summer Solstice 77
Mountain Lion 80
June Garden & Landscape 82
Foraged Plant: Lamb's-quarter (*Chenopodium album*) 83
Rewilding Ourselves 84
June Summary 87
Journaling Prompts for Self-Reflection 88

JULY

Poem: Fairy Dance 89
Intensity, Summer Heat & Outdoor Life. 89
Sun Gods. 90
Wild Turkey 92
July Garden & Landscape 94
Foraged Plant: Wild Bergamot (*Monarda fistulosa*). 95
Injuries, Insect Bites & Other Maladies 97
July Summary. 99
Journaling Prompts for Self-Reflection 100

AUGUST

Poem: Along the Road 101
Excess & Abundance 101
Grain Mothers & Corn Gods. 102
Snake 105
August Garden & Landscape. 107
Foraged Plant: Elderberry (*Sambucus species*) 108
Gift & Barter Economies. 109
August Summary 113
Journaling Prompts for Self-Reflection 113

SEPTEMBER

Poem: Autumn Meadow. 115
Harvesting, Sacred Pause 115
Fall Equinox & Harvest Festivals 118
Spider 120
September Garden & Landscape 122
Foraged Plant: Goldenrod (*Solidago species*). 124
What Is Enough? 125
September Summary 128
Journaling Prompts for Self-Reflection 128

OCTOBER

Poem: Essence 131
Ancestral Connections, Releasing 131
Samhain, Halloween & Day of the Dead 133

Squirrel 134
October Garden & Landscape 138
Foraged Plant: Hawthorn (*Crataegus species*) 139
Death & Dying in Nature 141
October Summary. 143
Journaling Prompts for Self-Reflection 144

NOVEMBER

Poem: Descent 145
Darkening of Days, Winter's Doorstep 145
The Dark Goddess: The Cailleach, Baba Yaga, Oya. 147
Crow/Raven 149
November Garden & Landscape 151
Foraged Plant: American Witch Hazel (*Hamamelis virginiana*) . 152
Creating Sanctuary & Winter Comfort 154
November Summary 157
Journaling Prompts for Self-Reflection 157

DECEMBER

Poem: Winter Solstice. 159
Wintering & Winter Solstice. 159
Deer & Reindeer Goddesses 162
Deer 164
December Garden & Landscape 166
Foraged Plant: Pine (*Pinus species*) 167
Honoring Liminal Space. 169
December Summary. 171
Journaling Prompts for Self-Reflection 172

Endnotes 173
Selected Bibliography 189
Acknowledgments 193
About the Author 195
About Bold Story Press. 197

INTRODUCTION

I never expected to come face-to-face with a mountain lion in my driveway or to save the life of a snake writhing in my hands. I had camped and hiked in the wilderness, learned primitive survival skills, and persevered through vision quests. I have always been a nature lover. But when I moved to the Virginia Highlands, I was not prepared for the true wildness of nature and the challenges to my urbanized, overeducated ways of being in the world.

As a young teen growing up in Germany, I kept a notebook with magazine snippets about animals, flowers, star constellations, and countries I wanted to visit. I vividly remember one black-and-white photo of an older woman in her kitchen garden surrounded by herbs, roses, and foxglove. While I longed to escape my rural village and my parents' working-class life, I loved that photo. It became my North Star even as the memory of the photo went dormant for a long time.

Over the course of three decades, I traveled across five continents, emigrated to the US, attended graduate school in Cincinnati, and established a career as a clinical psychologist in Washington, DC. This is where I raised my daughter, bought my first house, and created a little garden. I divorced and remarried. Despite frequent nature outings to the DC Metro area's many parks and green spaces, I kept yearning for a deeper immersion in nature. My daughter graduated from high school and pursued her own life. After my new husband retired early, we started daydreaming about moving to the country and trying our hands at homesteading. Soon we found an inexpensive piece of land in the remote Allegheny Highlands of Virginia and left it all behind—the city, the traffic, tidy suburban homes. In the meantime, both my husband's children and my daughter made us grandparents. Now, I have become that grandmother in the photo who tends to her gardens nestled into a mountain landscape.

This book is about my reconnection with nature and my desire to understand my place in the world by learning from the land I live on, the fifty-eight acres of hilly meadows and forests in the Virginia Highlands that my husband, Dan, and I call home. Dan and I now belong to the minority of humans who do not live in or near a city. More than half the world's population lives in urbanized areas. In the wealthiest parts of the world (western Europe, the Americas, the Middle East, Japan, and Australia), more than 80 percent of us live in cities,[1] distanced from the wild spaces and rural settings of our ancestors.

In the course of this massive urbanization, most people have lost firsthand knowledge of the interconnectedness between caring for the soil and caring for the health of the people, between the cycles and rhythms of nature and our own mental and spiritual well-being. This crisis of disconnection weaves through all parts of our world, fueling the destruction of nature spaces and ecosystems. It draws ever sharper demarcations between rich and poor and forces waves of climate-related migration and the associated political grandstanding, tightening of borders, and compassion fatigue. It pits environmental defenders against those unwilling to adapt their planet-warming lifestyles and those who continue to exploit natural resources and pollute the planetary commons.

All living beings evolved from a common universal ancestor, a single-celled organism, several billion years ago. We share 98.9 percent of our genetic material with chimps and up to 70 percent with trees. The bronchioles in our lungs have the same fractal pattern as tree branches or the dendrite channels of a river delta. Nature has always been part of us, and we have always belonged to her: just take a look at our myths and legends, our concepts of the divine, how our bodies are affected by the moon and sun, our fears of the dark or of snakes, our metaphors, our imagination, our yearnings for beauty and belonging.

Sitting with this dichotomy between our deep bond with nature and our painful separation from it, I have been wrestling with the question: How have we lost our connection, and how can we reclaim it?

This book is my attempt to answer that question.

Seasons of a Wild Life braids together what the land has taught me, from the nature forces that shape it, the animals that inhabit it, and the wild and cultivated plants that make themselves at home on our land, to the skills and practices I have acquired in the process of taking care of this property. I weave daily experiences on our farm with nature myths from my European roots and other cultures. Mythology and symbolism help us tap into our collective unconscious, the deep knowledge humans have gathered since we learned to use fire, tools, and language.

Seasons of a Wild Life moves through the calendar year from January to December. In each chapter, you will meet deities personifying nature's forces that month, from frost giants to the Grain Mother. You will learn about nature celebrations still observed around the world, from the winter solstice to ancient Beltane merriment to harvest festivals. You will meet the animals that live in our mountain environment—bear, snake, deer, spider—and learn about their habits and cultural symbolism. You will meander through garden and landscape witnessing the frosty, fallow land in winter, the exuberant eruption of the life force in spring, and the voluptuous abundance of autumn. You will learn about wild plants that offer beauty, food, and medicine, from stinging nettle to elderberry to witch hazel. You may feel inspired to learn a new skill or embrace a concept that connects earth-friendly practices to the challenges facing us as a world community.

If you are an urban dweller, it is important to realize that nature isn't only wild spaces and rural settings. Nature is all around us, as close as the ground under our feet, the oak tree in the park, weeds covering an abandoned lot, or hawks nesting on high-rise buildings bordering Central Park in New York City.

I hope *Seasons of a Wild Life* encourages you to apprentice yourself to whatever environment you find yourself in, and that you allow yourself to be nourished, enchanted, and more rooted by the place you inhabit.

I offer *Seasons of a Wild Life* in the spirit of healing: may we recognize our deeper purpose of being and nudge our inner nature toward a more conscious reconnection with nature around us.

JANUARY

Bare Bones

Frozen night
Slides into hazy blues

Trees and grasses
Holding in
Standing firm
Stiff outer armor
Soft dreaming inward

Waiting
      Knowing
            Waiting

Bare bones survival
Holding on
Standing tough
Stiff outer armor
Soft dreaming inward

Waiting
      Knowing
            Waiting

This, too, shall pass.

Incubation

Darkness and incubation meander through the month of January. Little observable activity takes place in the natural environment. With the ground frozen, often covered with snow and ice, outdoor activity is stifled. The garden is sleeping. Cold weather keeps me inside, where the woodstove spreads its dry warmth. When temperatures dip below zero degrees Fahrenheit, the ceiling timbers creak and crack as they contract with the cold. The wooden deck outside occasionally releases a startling gunshot noise. When the wind howls and rattles the house during these long, cold January nights, I am grateful for a cozy, secure home and food in the pantry and freezer.

After a fresh snowfall, when the sun sprinkles sparkly glitter across the land and the bluest sky highlights the untouched whiteness of the snowy landscape, I must go outside. Who can withstand this kind of magic: the hushed silence, the crispness of the air, the brightness of snow reflecting light even at night? Such primeval purity helps me get through this otherwise barren wintertime.

Clearing the snow from the porch, walkways, and cars, and plowing the quarter-mile driveway down to the main road then become the activities for the day, reddening my cheeks and filling me with a sense of accomplishment.

On most January days, however, Nature invites us to hold still, breathe, dream, look inward, and explore the darkness and depth of our being. Light and clarity hide somewhere in the undefined future. Do we dare surrender to this invitation? What might we find?

For many of us, this space of non-doing is contrary to our Western cultural training which calls for action, "getting something done." How often do we override midwinter's invitation to rest deeply and, instead, forge ahead with our New Year's plans, ignoring our winter fatigue, lights blazing into the night?

I struggle with non-doing, but I am tempted to heed winter's invitation. I am curious about what happens when I allow my linear, goal-setting left brain to take a break; when I put down my internal mental whip that demands obedience to my to-do list; when I consciously lean into each day, breathing through the gray, dark time.

David Whyte talks about the nature and necessity of *hiding*, the need to close ourselves off from outside influences, in line with the practices of the natural world during wintertime: "Hiding is creative, necessary and beautifully subversive of outside interference and control."[1] By hiding, we give ourselves the opportunity to reflect undisturbed, to allow what's incubating inside of us to fully form before we release it into the world. I think of a bear safely ensconced in an earth hollow, her cubs growing inside her womb. I think of my house as the firm membrane of my winter cocoon. Incubation and gestation occur best in the dark and must not be disturbed.

At the end of January, by sheer grace, a subtle shift happens: I wake up more alert with new ideas and energy. Mama Bear is sniffing the brisk air wafting into her hideaway.

Winter Deities & Frost Giants

The threat of freezing or starving to death permeated the winter season for our ancestors. In all parts of the world where cold winters occur, people turned the sometimes beautiful but often deadly forces of nature into supernatural figures.

Nordic myths describe frost giants who lived in the territories of Jotunheim. These ice giants were the first beings and had to be defeated by the gods before they were able to establish Aesir, their own home, the land of the gods. The frost giants were mostly hostile, but some of their women were incomparably beautiful. One of these alluring frost giantesses, Gerd, was richly covered in jewels that glittered in the sunlight like a pristine winter landscape.[2]

Finnish legends tell of a three-hundred-year-old snow king named Snaer, who himself was the son of Iceberg and who fathered three girls named Thick Snow, Snowstorm, and Fine Snow.[3] One of my favorite images depicting the harsh power of winter comes from Russia, where the blacksmith Moroz (Father Frost) encircles land and sea with his chains of ice.[4]

The Japanese describe a beautiful young snow maiden called Yuki Onna who wields winter's deadly powers in a deceptively gentle manner. When she encounters travelers during a snow-storm, she lulls them to sleep, then freezes them to death with her icy breath.[5]

In a similar manner, the Lakota winter giant, Waziya, invites human visitors to smoke a pipe with him, then casts his spell, freezing them to death. Waziya presents as an old man with a beard of icicles who is covered in wolf skins. He lives in an icy teepee in the skies. From his lofty abode, he commands the aurora borealis and sends forth the brutal north winds that spread snow and ice across the lands.[6]

Even Hawaii has a snow deity. A folktale describes how Poli-ahu, the resident snow goddess on the volcano Mauna Kea, wins a sled race against the fire goddess, Pele. After Pele loses the race, she wants revenge and reaches for Poliahu with her fiery lava fingers. However, the snow goddess quickly throws her mantle of snow over Pele's mountain and turns her hot lava into cold stone, blocking off the exit points from her volcano.[7]

Bear

During the early years on our mountain property in the Virginia Highlands, I was petrified of bears, though clueless about the origin of my fear. I was told that bears are scared of humans and will avoid us, unless cornered and in need of protecting their cubs. Just in case, I took my bear spray along when walking alone.

A few years ago, I visited a nature preserve in nearby West Virginia. Even though it was late in the afternoon and I still had a long drive home, I wanted to check quickly on the bog orchids and pitcher plants that are unique to that area. All other visitors had left already. It was eerily quiet, which should have tipped me off. When I heard a strange snorting, I was hoping it had come from a deer. But then the black furry shape of a bear rose on its hind legs behind a nearby bush. It took every ounce of willpower to slowly back away instead of running. When I finally reached the safety of my car, my heartbeat gradually returned to normal.

Following this encounter, I remembered a recurrent childhood nightmare of a large bear on his hind legs trying to push open the door to my room. I would wake up in terror, turned around in my bed and so spatially disoriented that I could not find my way around my room in the dark. Once I made the connection between my childhood dreams and my fear of bears, this fear gradually diminished.

The black bears that populate the eastern part of the US do not truly hibernate in winter, but enter a state of reduced activity called *torpor*, a perfect term for January's theme of cocooning and going inward. The need for honoring the dark and allowing transformation to occur in that hidden, fertile ground has ancient roots in the mythological stories of the bear. Bear mythology is prominent in northern countries around the world, including Siberian, Alaskan and other Indigenous American, Scandinavian, Celtic, and Germanic cultures. The bear may have been worshipped already by Neanderthal people, later followed by most arctic cultures and the indigenous people of Japan, the Ainu. Sometimes the bear was seen as the ancestor of humans; at other times, the bear became the powerful companion animal of the Great Goddess.[8]

The female bear has been widely regarded as a symbol of maternal strength, care, and protection. Old European and Native American traditions deeply honor and invoke the bear's ability to awaken the force of the unconscious. For Native Americans, the bear's hibernation in a cave symbolizes the Great Void. This space of inner knowing is also known as the Dream Lodge.[9]

In contrast, the masculine aspects of the bear are unmistakably aggressive and often deadly. In Scandinavia, the bear impersonates a fierce masculine force and is associated with Odin, supreme god of Nordic mythology. Viking warriors wore bear skins into battle. Raging men called "berserkers," derived from the root word for *bear*, committed atrocious acts of cruelty and destruction.

Both the terrifying and the introspective aspects of bear have shown up in my personal experience as well.

We occasionally see bears on our property, mostly at a distance. One night, though, I heard noise on our porch. Peeking through the window of our front door, I saw a bear eating from the cat bowl. His massive black shape filled the porch. Barely breathing, I watched him carry away the metal canister in which we store extra cat food. The next morning, I found first the lid, then the metal can near the edge of the woods; all of the cat food was gone. When the same bear returned to our porch the next night, the cat food was stored securely inside. I opened the door and yelled at him, then threw a shoe in his direction. He took his time leaving, looking back at me a few times before he ambled off into the woods, as if to say, "How dare this human deprive me of an easy dinner?"

It felt cathartic to chase the thieving bear away. A bit of self-righteous indignation helped to fuel my courage. After releasing the threatening bear from my childhood nightmares, real-life bears are no longer bloodthirsty monsters to my subconscious mind, but instead just one of the many wild animals we share our land with.

January Garden & Landscape

The frozen ground yields very little food, wild or cultivated. I might come across a few shriveled rosehips, barberries, or chokeberries still dangling from bare branches, if the birds have not found them yet. Pine and spruce needles make a delightful tea but provide few food calories.

In the garden, deep freezes wiped out my cold-hardy broccoli and kale by mid-December. But inside my hoop house (a small, unheated greenhouse), young kale, curly radish, and emerald green lettuce defy winter. After finding evidence of hungry critter activity, I set a mousetrap smeared with peanut butter and toss cotton balls soaked with peppermint and eucalyptus oils among my plants. The strong scent supposedly deters varmints. Sadly, both methods fail miserably, and my kale, spinach, and lettuce babies are ruthlessly devoured. The mousetrap remains untouched and the cotton balls continue to perfume the hoop house. Initially, I blame chipmunks or mice for this debauchery. After spotting a few large holes in the ground, I now suspect a big fat toad that is probably overwintering in this protected space. Toads are good allies in the garden; I don't want to kill it.

I give up on my winter harvest for now.

In the chilled landscape, pussy willows dot their branches with soft, silvery catkins. Everything else is bare winter bones: tree trunks and branches, shrubs, dried stalks of grasses and wildflowers. While I study their naked shapes, textures, and subtle colors, my eyes light up with the deep red of Osier dogwood branches and the singing orange of invasive Japanese barberries and oriental bittersweet. Their bright colors interrupt the bland winter palette of gray, white, brown, and muted conifer green, whispering promises.

Back in December, I clipped a few dormant forsythia branches and placed them in a vase filled with water. By late January, they have erupted into yellow sunshine blossoms. I sprinkle some of them on red sauerkraut served on green lettuce leaves. The contrasting colors on my dinner plate are one of the small delights that shepherd me through the barrenness of winter.

FORAGED PLANT
Jerusalem Artichoke (*Helianthus tuberosus*)

These are lean times for foraging outside the pantry or a grocery store. The single reliable wild food source now, if the ground isn't frozen solid, is my Jerusalem artichoke patch.

Jerusalem artichoke, also called sunchoke, is a native sunflower that can grow six to eight feet tall in rich soil. In August, each hairy stalk, covered with coarse, dark green leaves, produces a multitude of small sunflowers. The flowers do not produce any edible seeds. Instead, its food value is hidden in the ground. The mild-tasting tubers, tan-colored and bulbous, resemble ginger root. The tubers can be boiled and smothered in butter or sliced or grated raw into salads. A friend pickles them and gifted me with a jar, a rare delicacy. Sunchokes contain high levels of inulin which can cause flatulence. Soaking the chopped tubers in water and vinegar before cooking seems to minimize that unpleasant side effect.

What gardener isn't fond of plants that require little to no work? Jerusalem artichokes are virtually effortless to grow and maintenance-free. Simply toss a few tubers in the ground in late fall or early spring, then wait for them to grow. The flowers create a riotous hedge of sunny yellow flowers. They will spread exuberantly, so think carefully about where you want to plant them. The tubers can be harvested any time after the first frost and into early spring.

Winter foraging reminds me of the hardships our ancestors endured while trying to survive a long winter, before grocery stores offered strawberries from Peru or avocados from Mexico in January. So it is with quiet joy and humble gratitude that I collect food from my land in the middle of winter.

Mending & Repair

Mending and repairing are primarily indoor activities, something we can do even as a blizzard howls outside. To me, these are useful and satisfying activities that help minimize cabin fever and combat seasonal depression. They keep things out of landfills and money in our pockets. They save valuable resources that might have been used for a new item and avoid some of the environmental and human costs associated with so many single-use products made today. Mending helps me to slow down and focus on a single task, gifting me with the opportunity for a mindful working meditation.

In addition to mending clothing or repairing broken objects, winter is also the perfect time for self-care and body repair. This is the time when I open my pantry for the herbal treasures

I gathered during the previous growing season. There are mason jars filled with dried herbs alongside brown bottles protecting plant medicine infused into vodka tinctures. During these frozen-cold times, sage, mullein, coltsfoot, bee balm, and holy basil are favored plant allies. Teas and facial steams concocted from these herbs are reliable home remedies for winter colds and respiratory infections. Salves with comfrey, plantain, and calendula ease dry and cracked skin on elbows, hands, and feet.

Our ancestors spent wintertime mending quilts and articles of clothing, carding and spinning wool into yarn; cleaning, sharpening, and repairing tools; and crafting new clothing and tools. I imagine them sitting around the woodstove or fireplace sipping tea or spiced wine and working away in silence, bits of conversation bubbling up occasionally.

Even in our modern times, January remains a good month for repair work that has piled up through the year. I sew patches on Dan's favorite work pants and jackets to give them a few more seasons of wear. As a bonus, these patches give him street credibility as a working man in our rural county. Local farmers, who barely exchanged a greeting for the first ten years of our time in the county, now are chatty with him. I think my patches may have had something to do with it.

Woodstove heat takes a toll on wood and leather, so I refurbish our living room furniture by cleaning the leather upholstery with a damp cloth, then rubbing leftover homemade salve into it. I figure what's good for human skin, a concoction of beeswax and herb-infused olive oil, will work on animal skin as well. The salve smooths over the tiny dry cracks in the leather, which, after some polishing action, once again radiate a pleasing soft sheen.

My husband fixes a leaking pipe leading to our water heater. This is not a quick and easy chore but an afternoon's commitment to first identify the exact nature of the problem (a worn-out rubber washer), locate a replacement part, and put everything back together. Luckily, the local hardware store had the washer in stock. When spare parts are not available in our remote area, a long drive to the Shenandoah Valley or into West Virginia is required. Lots of things can and do go wrong on a homestead, and I am grateful for all the do-it-yourself (DIY) skills we share between the two of us. If neither one of us can fix it, we can usually find someone in the community with the necessary expertise.

I enjoy watching the British TV show *The Repair Shop*. Here, customers bring in family heirlooms that often seem beyond repair. *The Repair Shop* employees have highly specialized skills in porcelain, upholstery, cane, and metalwork; they are a rare breed of humans nowadays. When a faded antique chair has been restored or a broken porcelain figure repaired and repainted to its former glory, customers' faces light up. They leave the shop smiling, cradling their treasured item that may connect them to a beloved grandparent.

It makes sense to invest energy and expense into repairing an item that not only holds emotional significance but was made with quality materials by skilled artisans. We would not be tempted to invest the same energy into fixing a dollar-store object made from cheap plastic or pressed plywood that falls apart after a short period of use.

Those of us raised in a planned-obsolescence economy often throw away products that are still perfectly good or that only require minor repair. These are just a few examples I gleaned from an employee at our local landfill: One man dropped off a brand-new raccoon trap complaining that it didn't work. But the trap worked perfectly in the hands of someone who actually knew how to set it. Somebody else unloaded a refrigerator with a few dents on the outside but otherwise in perfect working condition. A floor fan only needed a bit of tinkering to be functional again.

Many communities have created buy/sell/swap sites on social media such as Buy Nothing groups on Facebook, where people give away unwanted items. No money or bartering involved.

Judging from the popularity of DIY YouTube videos, people do want to learn how to repair something or acquire other handy skills. Would you like to know how to slaughter a goose? Do you need highly detailed repair instructions for your off-road motorcycle or down-draft stove? Do you want to learn how to sew or knit or make paper from scratch? Well, there's a YouTube video for it!

Perhaps this interest in online DIY tutorials was prompted by the economic recession in 2008 and, more recently, by the constraints imposed by the COVID-19 pandemic. Diminished income levels for many, a greater awareness of the environmental and human impact of thoughtless disposal of items, greater access to video-making technology—all these factors contribute to an increased interest in mending and repairing as components of a larger arsenal of self-reliance and do-it-yourself skills.

A growing number of repair cafés, tool libraries, online swap sites, and mutual aid societies are hopeful indicators that we are beginning to value things and people in a new way.

Why *do* we repair, and what is the value of repair? In her book *Repair*, Elizabeth Spelman states: "To repair is to acknowledge and respond to the fracturability of the world."[10] Perhaps we restore a sense of wholeness, of how we think the world should be, when we repair something that is broken. Beyond the obvious benefits of restoring broken items, the habit of mending and repairing things has larger ripple effects.

I find myself slowing down when I make time to darn a hole in my favorite wool socks, sew a button back on a sweater, or turn an old bed sheet into handkerchiefs or bandanas. It allows me to think about the effort it took to source the basic materials these objects were made from, the people who were involved in crafting the products, and the people who taught me the skills to maintain and repair these objects with a sense of appreciation.

Mending and repairing are activities embedded in a larger worldview that values the interconnectedness of resources, humans, and environment. In an encouraging recent development, France has pioneered subsidies to businesses specializing in repairs to encourage French consumers to have their clothing and shoes mended professionally. This initiative aims to accomplish two goals: to preserve jobs requiring traditional craftsmanship and to extend the life of garments and footwear, which make up a substantial portion of landfill trash.[11]

Perhaps one of the most beautiful approaches to repairing objects that combines functionality and an underlying philosophy of life can be found in the Japanese custom *kintsugi*. Repair of a broken porcelain or pottery item is not accomplished by trying to hide the broken places but instead by embellishing and highlighting the mended places with gold. *Kintsugi* is an offspring of the Japanese philosophy of *wabi-sabi*, which finds beauty in imperfection as well as *mottainai*, which seeks to avoid wastefulness.[12]

There is great satisfaction in making something whole again, and it may just transfer to other areas of our lives that need restoration and healing: relationships, watersheds, abandoned lots.[13]

January Summary

The first month of the year offers an opportunity to tend to our inner world. When we hold still and listen inward, we may catch glimpses of the gifts hidden inside this cold, dark time of confinement. Many of us create New Year's resolutions only to abandon them by February when that brand-new energy tends to fizzle out. Can we instead create space to reflect undisturbed, to listen to our inner bear's snoring and gentle stirrings? And while we wait for the birth of our New Year self, we might as well find something for our hands to do: knit a hat, sew a broken hem, darn some favorite wool socks, write those letters we've been wanting to write, make that phone call we've been putting off, fix something that's broken. We want to be ready for the bear to emerge from its winter cave with new energy, fresh ideas, and restored hope.

Writing Prompts for Self-Reflection

1. Do you have a practice of silence? What does it look like?

2. How can you bring more stillness and restfulness into your life during the darkest months?

3. What internal and external distractions prevent you from experiencing stillness?

4. What needs mending or repair in your life (objects, relationships, personal issues, social/cultural/ political issues)?

5. What needs decluttering in your life, both physically and emotionally?

6. What is incubating for you right now?

FEBRUARY

Winter's Tail

Wind howls through the night
Rattles winter's icy hold
Thin robins return.

Resilience

February's guiding theme of resilience captures the task of making it through another winter. This was a particularly challenging month for our ancestors, as the "hunger gap" stretched from this midwinter time of dwindling food supplies to the appearance of the first garden crops, still a few months away.

February is an unpredictable month here in the Virginia Highlands. Some days, winter seems to strengthen its icy grip, as temperatures can dip lower than in January. Other days feel like spring and invite us outside even as last year's grass remains brown and lifeless. Energetically, a subtle but noticeable shift has occurred. As the days are getting longer ever so gradually, the sun grows stronger, buds begin to swell, bird song and activity increase. A bluebird couple inspects the bluebird house during the middle of the month, and a kestrel sits in the tree next to the kestrel box. Spring is close now. My mood and energy levels are rising.

The bird feeder serves as a source of daily entertainment. I notice a sparrow-like bird with a small red patch on its head and faint red streaks on its breast, and wonder whether it might be an early-arrival finch. Thumbing through my bird books, I identify the stranger as a common redpoll, a bird I have never seen before. No wonder, because this bird is thousands of miles from its usual Arctic habitat. The birds I expect to see around my feeder include the familiar cardinal, chickadee, titmouse, nuthatch, junco, blue jay, various sparrows, and woodpeckers. The redpoll disappears after a few weeks; its visitation remains one of nature's mysteries.

Taking a walk around my property, I am delighted by the many different shapes of icicles hanging like spiky or bulbous glass ornaments from tree branches, grasses, even the clothesline. Icicles drop from trees and splinter across the snow crust like breaking glass. Long, thin pieces of ice that have formed along horizontal fence wires pivot slightly and for a few moments hang vertically like perfect glass straws before dropping to the ground.

What I love most of all is the sound of dripping ice. After the hushed tranquility of snow-covered land, the sound of melting ice is quite noisy. The pervasive drip-dripping creates its own music, the music of life awakening and impending change. These tiny ecstatic moments of winter beauty brushed with the faintest hint of spring define the essence of February.

Brigid

Our northern hemisphere ancestors were intensely attuned to the earliest inklings of spring and the accompanying energetic shift that occurs in early February, the midpoint between the winter solstice and the spring equinox. European festivals of lights include Imbolc, St. Brigid's Day, Candlemas, and Feast of the Presentation. The modern observance of Groundhog Day in the United States appears to be a paltry remnant of such celebrations, perhaps with ancient roots in badger and bear cults.

Imbolc is a feast dedicated to the Celtic goddess Brigid, and dates back to Neolithic times, the late Stone Age period when humans established large settlements, domesticated animals, and developed agriculture. Beginning in the Bronze Age (3300–1200 BCE), the Celts built megalithic monuments in Brigid's honor. The Hill of Tara in Ireland is an ancient ceremonial and burial site and only one example of the massive earthworks and stone constructions found throughout the Celtic world. The main stone structure of the Hill of Tara is architecturally and astronomically aligned in such a way that on Imbolc morning the light of the rising sun shines through a special opening in the stone.[1]

Brigid worship was widespread throughout the Celtic world, which included Ireland, the Scottish Highlands and islands, the Isle of Man, and western Europe. Brigid's ancient Gaelic name was Breo-Saighead, which translates into fiery power or fiery arrow. She has been depicted with rays of light radiating out from her head, possibly reflecting her status as protector of the hearth fire as well as the blacksmith's forge. Wearing many hats, Brigid was also the goddess of the healing arts and of wells, which were considered sacred emissions from the earth.[2]

During Imbolc, people celebrated when cows and sheep started birthing their young and the first swelling of spring buds promised new growth. To ensure fertility and abundance in the coming season, offerings of food reminiscent of the color of the sun, such as milk, butter, eggs, and honey, were prepared. Because Brigid represented the part of the year that ended the cold, dark days of winter, Imbolc was also a celebration of light and warmth amplified by bonfires, hearth fires, and lit candles.[3]

The traditions connected to Brigid honor domestic chores ordinarily performed by women. To prepare for Imbolc, women cleaned their homes and took stock of dwindling food supplies left in their cupboards and cellars.[4] This is probably where our modern rite of spring cleaning has its origins. Some of us still instinctively respond to the lengthening of days and the first ever-so-subtle signs of spring by cleaning and readying our living space for a new season.

Here in the Virginia Highlands, February is lambing and calving season. Young calves and tiny lambs on skinny legs stagger behind their mothers on pastures still dotted with snowy patches. February is also prime season for maple syrup production. The rising sap collected from maple trees is boiled down into sweet syrup. With its golden color, maple syrup could easily qualify as an Imbolc food.

Owl

A barred owl appeared to me on the first day of February. As I was driving into town, I saw it sitting on a tree close to the road. To my surprise, the owl was still in the same spot when I returned from my errands. I sent a silent greeting and knew that it had now become this month's featured animal.

I rarely see owls. They are well camouflaged and might sit in a tree above, entirely unnoticed. Owls tend to be nocturnal and use their voices to mark territory and to attract and communicate with mates. Some owl species begin mating and nesting during midwinter and can be heard during this time of year. I have heard their rhythmic, almost ominous hooting at night. Among the eight owls most commonly found in Virginia, there is a vast repertoire of owl voices, from the hissing sound of a barn owl, the I-cook-for-you, I cook-for-you-all pronouncements of the barred owl, to the eerie whinnying of the eastern screech owl. Sometimes, I find the regurgitated remnants of an owl's meal—a few feathers from a smaller bird, bits of fur from a small mammal. Mostly, owls remain elusive.

Owls are powerful birds of prey with highly sensitive hearing and excellent eyesight. They hunt noiselessly at night, swooping down on mice, voles, and small birds and eating them whole. They regurgitate the indigestible parts of their prey. Owls claim the entire world as their territory and can be found on all continents except Antarctica. They have settled into vastly different habitats from suburbia and farms to forests, from high deserts and arctic zones to tropical regions.[5]

The Neolithic eye goddess (also called bird goddess) had heavily emphasized owl eyes. Her intense and unblinking stare symbolized her ability to look into both the visible and the invisible worlds. The bird goddess was also depicted in highly stylized form as a double spiral.[6] While the most well-known double spiral is engraved at the Newgrange burial site in Ireland, the eye goddess's insignia have also been found in burial grounds on the Mediterranean islands of Malta and Crete and many countries across Europe. The Basque goddess Mari and the Baltic owl goddess Ragana are examples of ancient European bird goddesses. Ragana was sacred to women and presided over important life phases, including childbirth, menstruation, and menopause. Babylonians depicted Lilith as a beautiful winged goddess with bird feet and claws. In Christian times, Lilith became a demonic figure, and Ragana was turned into a witch. Mari disappeared into the shadows of prehistory.[7,8]

Since ancient times, birds, and especially owls, were seen as the messengers of the gods. As they were capable of flying from earth to the heavens, they became sacred guardians who accompanied deceased souls into the afterlife in many Middle Eastern cultures. In ancient Egypt, the owl signified night, death, and the realm of the dead.[9] The owl was also sacred to the ancient Sumerian goddess Inanna; to Athena, the Greek goddess of war, wisdom, and intellect;[10] and to the Hindu goddess of wealth and wisdom, Lakshmi.[11]

With the arrival of Christianity, owls and bird goddesses became associated with witches and black magic. The Old Testament labeled owls as unclean symbols of loneliness, mourning, and judgment. In modern-day Japan, on the other hand, owls are still used as lucky charms, offering protection from suffering.

My personal symbolic association to owls is partly a call to action—to wake up from my winter coma and pay close attention—and partly a nudge to trust my intuition and inner knowing. The owl reminds me to focus my energies inward and into my writings. The owl admonishes me to not get ruffled by external events, to safeguard my emotional energies instead of squandering them. I have a sudden insight this month that I am wasting emotional energy on yearning for what I can't have at the moment—sunshine, warmth, color. What else in my life am I resisting that is an exercise in futility? The guiding principle this month is resilience, which requires making peace with my current reality. That reality consists of facing the end of winter and preparing for spring without mentally escaping. Now is the time to build my internal stamina before flying out into the world with my vision and offerings for the year. Draw inward, consolidate, strengthen, refine: this is the owl's metaphysical message to me.

I also observe this month that my perceptions seem more attuned. As I watch a herd of nine deer that crosses our property every day, I am compelled to take out my binoculars and notice that the fully grown females all appear to be pregnant. The angled morning light emphasizes the roundedness of their bellies. This is not the case in the smaller, younger does. I don't remember ever noticing pregnant deer in the past. Perhaps owl with her keen eyesight nudged me into looking more closely?

The owl waiting for me by the side of the road on that first day of February broke winter's spell, in synchronistic time for Imbolc.

February Garden & Landscape

The still-dormant garden already invites brief spurts of labor. I remove the dried fronds of last season's asparagus, then weed and add compost to the patch that also hosts my strawberries. Hopefully, in another eight weeks, we will be rewarded with the first asparagus spears pushing up through the soil like little alien creatures.

My blueberry bushes require acidity to thrive, so I sprinkle an organic acidifying powder on the soil around each bush. This should have been done before winter to slowly trickle down to the roots, but I hope that even a late feeding will still support a bountiful blueberry harvest this year.

I prune my fruit trees, berry bushes, and some of the ornamental shrubs and save a few twigs to place in a vase inside the house. Within days, the magnolia buds show hints of their magenta-velvet blossoms preparing to unfurl. Pruning not only improves the health and production of trees but also makes me ponder other things that can be improved or refined by cutting away excess, materially, interpersonally, and spiritually. The garden is full of metaphors.

In my living room, several *Phalaenopsis* orchids reliably put out white and purple blooms that last all winter. The begonias I rescued from last fall's porch containers give me daily presents of red and pink flowers. A large flowerpot houses long, slender lemongrass leaves that make a delicately flavored tea. A few leftover tulip bulbs erupt into stately pink flowers, two months before their siblings would bloom outside. My houseplants inevitably lift my flagging winter spirits and are an essential part of my winter-survival toolkit.

Maple Syrup

Just when winter threatens to fray my last thinning thread of patience, Mother Nature is quietly working her magic. When the nights are still frozen but daytime temperatures climb above freezing, trees draw up moisture from the ground. Nobody really knows when humans first discovered that this rising tree water could be turned into delicious syrup. Native Americans crafted syrups from birch, walnut, and maple trees long before European settlers arrived.

While Canada and New England are the best-known and most prolific maple syrup producers, our own Highland County in Virginia is the southernmost location in the United States for maple syrup production.

As maple tree sap rises here during the month of February, the colorless, faintly sweet liquid is collected over a period of four to six weeks before the branches begin to bud and the sap takes on an unpleasant taste. Small holes are drilled into the tree bark and a spile, a small spigot, is inserted into the hole. This is called "tapping the trees." The rising tree water drips through the spile into an attached bucket or flows through plastic piping into large storage containers.

A vast network of plastic pipes connects hundreds of trees in the *sugar bush*, a stand of maple trees. These blue lines resemble gigantic spiderwebs suspended between the trees. At the sugar camps, the collected tree water is poured into oversized shallow metal pans and boiled down over a wood fire. Soon, sticky steam rises into the rafters of the sugar house. Forty gallons of tree sap yield one gallon of maple syrup.

Turning tree water into viscous, sweet syrup is both an art and a science. While hydrometers help determine the desired consistency, experienced syrup makers pay close attention to evaporating steam and bubbling action, often staying up through the night. If you fall asleep or get distracted by a chatty visitor, syrup can quickly turn into burnt crust. The desired end product of this alchemical food tradition is delicious syrup that varies in color from honeyed amber to dark molasses; the darker the color, the richer the taste. In our household, we use maple syrup to flavor a variety of foods ranging from granola, cakes, meats, and ice cream to milk shakes and coffee.[12]

So when you pick up a jar of real maple syrup at the grocery store, you may want to send out a thought of appreciation to all the hardworking people who labor in the woods and sugar camps to create this delectable food product for you. It truly is a labor of love. I have often fantasized about making our own maple syrup, but this remains a romantic concept. Realistically, we don't have the time, energy, or facilities to pull it off. So I gladly leave maple syrup production to the experienced old-timers.

Avoiding Food Waste

Especially during winter, I think about the Manahoacs and Monacans, Native Americans who lived in the Allegheny Mountains before Scots-Irish and German colonizers invaded and displaced them. Both Native Americans and settler pioneers were dependent on the food they gathered and stored during the growing season. Before the onset of global warming, winters here in the Appalachian Mountain Range were much harsher and lasted longer. Early February was the midpoint between the previous year's harvest and the first spring harvest. People still needed half of their stored food supplies for humans and animals to survive.

In February 2021, unusually cold winter weather occurred all the way into southern Texas, causing disruptions in electricity and water supply for millions of people who were unprepared for such extreme weather. Dozens froze to death in their own homes. Climate chaos is here to stay, and, as was mandatory for our ancestors, it would be wise even for us modern people to be prepared by stocking up on food and supplies and having alternate modes of generating electricity.

Humans in the modern world, however, mostly have the opposite challenge: instead of food scarcity, most of us face food waste even as there are millions of food-insecure people in the US and many more throughout the world. Food insecurity and food waste are issues at opposite poles of food accessibility. They require conscientious solutions that involve reducing food waste to decrease environmental pressures on land and water resources and to ensure that people who need food have access to it. What causes food waste and what can we, as consumers, do to avoid or minimize it?

We may not think that it is a big deal to throw a piece of moldy cheese, a few wilted greens, or the oozing mess that used to be a zucchini in the garbage. However, when we look at nationwide and worldwide statistics, food waste takes on massive proportions. Anne-Marie Bonneau, blogger at *The Zero-Waste Chef* and author of *The Zero Waste Chef: Plant-Forward Recipes and Tips for a Sustainable Kitchen and Planet*, sourced the following statistics from the National Resources Defense Council, Food and Agriculture Organization of the

United Nations, Project Drawdown, and *Scientific American*: on average, each American household wastes about one pound of food per day. When accounting for produce left behind in the fields, spoiled in storage or during transportation, and thrown away by supermarkets, restaurants and institutional settings, 40 percent of all food produced in the United States ends up as food waste. Worldwide, statistics are not much better: one-third of food generated ends up being thrown away. To make matters worse, when dumped into landfills, food breaks down anaerobically, releasing methane gas and producing 8 percent of all human-caused greenhouse emissions. In addition, the food we waste sucks up 21 percent of all the water used for agricultural purposes in the US.[13]

These are staggering numbers. Surely, with a bit of planning and awareness, we can all commit to reducing food waste in our own households. Here are some of Bonneau's suggestions:

- Determine the causes of food spoilage in your home and adjust your food buying and cooking accordingly.

- Use what is in the pantry and refrigerator first, before going grocery shopping. Avoid impulse buying by taking a shopping list along.

- Shop locally, and if possible, directly from farmers. In the US, you can also order from online produce suppliers like Imperfect Foods or Misfits Market that rescue foods rejected by supermarkets due to overly restrictive standards for size and appearance.

- Plan more than one meal, using up perishable food first; freeze extra meals or food that cannot be used immediately. Learn to store food properly. Preserve foods that cannot be eaten in time through pickling or fermenting, which increases not only their shelf life but also beneficial gut bacteria.

- Reuse leftovers: tonight's dinner becomes lunch the next day. This practice also decreases the amount of packaging and food waste generated by take-out food. Bring a reusable container for leftovers when you eat out.

- Compost food scraps.[14]

When I roast a chicken, the only unavoidable waste product is the plastic wrapper it came in, even when bought directly from the chicken farmer. The roasted chicken meat will be used for several meals. Our dogs and cats happily eat the undesirable parts such as cartilage and skin. I simmer the bones in water for twenty-four to thirty-six hours until the concoction yields a nutritious bone broth. I strain out the broth for use as soup base or for cooking rice, then turn the softened bones into bone mush in my Vitamix blender. The dogs love it.

In her book *An Everlasting Meal*, Tamar Adler offers reading pleasure along with a food philosophy that seeks to avoid waste. She transforms the humble act of shelling peas into a calming meditative act.[15] After shelling the peas, she simmers the pea pods into a nutritious soup base. As one of her strategies to use all parts of produce and meats, she suggests incorporating their *tail ends*: "The bones and shells and peels of things are where a lot of their goodness resides."[16] She reminds the reader that "at the bottom of any pot of vegetables or beans or grains or meat are unrepeatable flavors themselves, all the alchemy of today's cooking distilled into a liquid you can neatly pour into a glass jar."[17] This flavorful liquid, the tail end of today's meal, is used to season another meal. Adler expertly advises the reader on using inexpensive parts of an animal (which are often discarded) and dedicates an entire chapter to creatively rescuing food that is burnt, oversalted, or too spicy.

Inspired, I set up a Crock-Pot to make veggie broth with scraps gleaned from around my kitchen: scooped-out fibers and seeds from a winter squash, ends of celery sticks, celery leaves and parsley stems, a bundle of frozen grapevine leaves never used for their intended dolmas-making purpose, freshly trimmed ends of lemongrass leaves from my potted houseplant, and a handful of dried hawthorn berries sitting forlorn on the counter. After this concoction simmers away for an afternoon, I add pan juices from roasting sweet potatoes flavored with remnants of olive oil, rosemary, salt, pepper, and caramelized sweetness. I often save food scraps in the freezer until I have enough to cook them into a veggie broth. The strained remnants from this broth enrich the compost heap. Bonneau, the Zero-Waste Chef, has many creative suggestions for the use of such a broth, including as a base for cooking beans, rice, and spaghetti.[18]

I feel a deep sense of satisfaction, not just for the broth that contains valuable micronutrients extracted from food scraps, but because this frugal habit honors the survival skills and pragmatism of my parents and generations of farmers before them. As a child I was taught that food must never be wasted. A surplus of plums, strawberries, or peaches would be turned into jam or canned in sweet syrup for winter use. A wall of top-to-bottom shelves in the basement was filled with all manner of canned fruit and vegetables. A huge ceramic crock held large amounts of sauerkraut with its live beneficial bacterial cultures. Anything we could not eat ourselves went straight into the pig bucket or the compost pile in the garden. Not only was the idea of food waste heretical, but almost everyone also knew how to prepare inexpensive food in a variety of different ways. My mother turned humble potatoes into many tasty dishes: lard-fried cubed potatoes with a delicious crust, boiled potatoes with butter and parsley, potato pancakes, creamy potato soup, potato as a thickening agent in hearty stews, mashed potatoes, vinegary potato salad with hard-boiled eggs, potato bread with leftover mashed potatoes, and baked potatoes loaded with savory *quark* (a soft cheese) mixed with onions and chives. Learning how to use basic ingredients in multiple ways helps prevent food waste. In addition, Bonneau has suggestions for using food scraps that typically get thrown away, such as turning apple cores into vinegar or transforming stale bread into croutons or breadcrumbs.[19]

By not wasting any food, I am honoring my peasant ancestors who knew how to make do and used up every scrap. Food-wise practices also respect the hard labor of those who plant, harvest, and transport the produce we buy at the farmer's market or supermarket. I am keenly aware of how time and labor intensive it is to grow food in my own garden. It involves physical labor, almost daily tending, exposure to pests, wildlife, weather, and other influences that determine a successful harvest or a wasted effort. Even foraging for wild foods requires harvesting, cleaning, and processing in some manner.

February Summary

As winter drags on, I am irritable and restless with cabin fever. While I daydream of palm trees swaying at the edge of turquoise ocean water, I marvel at the winter trees here, seemingly unbothered, trunks and limbs fully exposed, and the wildflowers that abandoned all vanity and withdrew into their corms and tubers underground. Do they become impatient and rise up from the ground in protest of winter? Do the deer complain about the cold and crave tasty spring greens while searching for dried-up grasses underneath the snow? Of course not! Plants and animals alike are adapted and have refined their survival skills through eons of cold seasons.

Owl stares me down, unblinking and indifferent: you've got this. You have all the resources and comforts you need, including shelter, food, heat, inside light. The lack of outer movement has given me ample opportunities to delve into my inner landscape, to dive deeply into myth, story, and imagination, and to plan forward from that rich inner place. The owl reminds me that winter does not have to be my adversary. Its challenges can be reframed as invitations to hone my resilience, to rest deeply, to listen into non-doing and not-knowing.

Journaling Prompts for Self-Reflection

1. What are the very first signs of spring in your area? What energetic shifts do you notice within yourself?

2. Where do you see signs of resilience in nature? How would you describe your own resilient qualities?

3. What kind of self-care or nourishment do you need this month to address emotional, physical, or spiritual needs?

4. If you are not already doing this, what kind of celebration would you create for yourself to mark the early beginnings of spring? What kinds of foods, rituals, and/or images would be involved?

5. How do you express your creativity? Do you have a practice such as writing, music, dance, crafting? Do you garden or raise children? What do you want to create in this season of new beginnings?

6. Do owl's qualities of insight, perceptiveness, and powerful hunting skills resonate with you? In what ways?

MARCH

Morning Prayer

A newborn day,
damp with rolling fog
soon to rise
like smoky tongues
through baby blue air.

Sun Goddess,
as you birth this new day,
unveil the trees from
their night shadow,
slide your luminous fingers
into hidden hollows,
knead the hills into loaves of clay,
and warm their curves
with buttery kisses.

Resurrection of the Life Force

March is full of drastic changes as the life force returns in so
many manifestations now. I feel like a diver perched on a diving
board preparing to jump. Communally, we are eager to announce
newly hatched offerings, anxious to get out into the world, and
hopeful to connect with others. I have to resist the temptation to
fill my calendar with too many activities popping up now: spring
flower walks, plant and seed swaps, and other community celebrations. I want to do them all. I have spring fever.

These are some of the "firsts" I anticipate this month: first laundry on the clothesline, first gardening work, first foraged spring greens, first kestrel couple claiming the nesting box.

Each morning now, I step outside on the porch and listen. Birdsong in early spring revs up to a lively soundscape. Throughout winter, I heard the nasal muttering of white-breasted nuthatches, the loud cackling of woodpeckers, the insistent shriek of blue jays. In March, however, many migratory birds return and fill the morning air with their mating songs and the sheer exuberance of existence: robins, red-winged blackbirds, flycatchers looking for nesting places under our gutters, turkey vultures quietly circling high up in the air currents. When a melodious cadence rises among all the other voices, I know that meadowlarks are back. Their sweet song evokes a strange feeling of longing in me for something I cannot name.

Distinct and unique, each bird has its own language. Also, birds produce different sounds for different scenarios. When among themselves, just pecking away for food, they emit tiny sounds to let each other know where they are and that they are okay. Triumphant territorial sounds announce to the world that this is their place, and they have claimed it. Special mating sounds aim at winning over that lovely female in the next tree. Alarm calls signal that a predator was spotted and the unmistakable sounds of protest and horror when a mate or a baby bird is being attacked by a predator.[1]

A pair of eastern bluebirds has claimed the nesting box in the nearby wild cherry tree. The male's blue feathers covering his head, wings, and tail appear to have intensified into a more vivid color from a somewhat duller phase before mating season began. The female's coloring is always more muted, her blue often fading into gray, and her rust-colored underside also more subtle than her mate's. Currently, the bluebird couple's contented private chatter turns into sharp cries when an avian intruder occupies a branch above their nesting box. I watch them dive-bomb the starling with threatening noises, the equivalent of yelling in bird language. They successfully chase the starling away. A short while later, the starling returns with two mates for reinforcement. The bluebirds, each only about half the size of a starling, first scold them, then launch coordinated attacks until the challengers fly away for good. It is nest-building time for these bluebirds. They clean up last year's debris from their birdhouse and fly in fresh bits of dried grasses to create a comfortable hollow on top of the old nest. Together, they craft a proper bed for the eggs the female is already growing in her body.

Here in the Virginia Highlands, we have entered the bipolar phase of late winter and early spring: rapid fluctuations between the first joyous signs of spring and another snowstorm. Thankfully, these late-winter storms tend to be brief events, as the sun now quickly melts any snow accumulation. Iris and daffodil leaves pop back up, undeterred by the transient snow cover and determined to fulfill their spring mandate.

My special treat in early March when the mountains are still clinging to winter is a visit to a nearby arboretum in the Shenandoah Valley (aka the Valley). Even though the Valley is only one hour's drive away, the climate is milder there, inviting flowers to bloom a few weeks earlier than they do in the Highlands.

At the arboretum, you hear traffic and construction noise even when you move deeper into the woodlands. Still, this place is my early-spring sanctuary, where I greet things green and flowering to soothe my cabin fever.

What I see at the arboretum signals the beginning of the spring intoxication soon to appear in the Highlands: dangly snowdrops, hellebores with dark red petal skirts, cheery golden winter aconite, yellow and red witch hazel flowers, dark purple dwarf iris with bold yellow patches, and the very first magenta flowers on an azalea bush. Pure, luscious eye candy. This outing nourishes me deeply. Now I can return home and wait a few more weeks for our mountains to adorn themselves in a similar fashion. By late March, the sunshine yellow of daffodils delights my color-starved eyes. I bring a bouquet inside and drink in its luminous color with my morning coffee. Spring is finally here; my body relaxes, and my breathing deepens a little.

The spring equinox on March 21–22 marks the halfway point between the shortest day of the year in December and the longest day in June. During the spring equinox, night and day are of equal length, darkness and light in balance. Soon, light outpaces the dark, sparking the expansive spring energy we know so well.

Frost Giants & Sun Gods

The Nordic tales of the frost giantesses and their initial resistance to and eventual marriage to the sun gods perfectly capture the push-pull dynamic during March's transition from winter to spring.

According to legend, the young, handsome god, Frey, was the personification of spring. After falling in love with Gerd, a gorgeous frost giantess, Frey sent his servant to woo Gerd with gifts of apples and a golden ring. Gerd made Frey wait for nine months (the duration of the northern winter) before agreeing to marry. The marriage of Frey and Gerd likely symbolized the sun's power to melt snow and winter yielding to the much-anticipated summer warmth.[2]

Native Americans also personified the interplay of winter and spring forces. In Algonquin myth, the Summer Elf spread warmth across the earth after defeating the Winter Giant. In Pueblo legend, the Winter Spirit Shakok and the Summer Spirit Miochin battled over Yellow Woman, the corn goddess, also called Corn Maiden. After a fierce fight involving lightning and icy winds, they came to an agreement: Shakok would be married to Yellow Woman in fall and winter. During that time, the corn stopped growing. Miochin, who ruled the warmer seasons, would be married to her during spring and summer when the corn started growing again.[3] These Native American myths of the battling seasons are very similar to the Greek legend in which Hades, god of the underworld, holds Persephone, the daughter of Demeter, goddess of agriculture and fertility, prisoner each winter. While Persephone remains in the underworld, Demeter mourns her daughter's absence, causing all vegetation to die. Everything comes to life again when Persephone is released in the spring.[4]

After prolonged battles with the various frost, ice, and snow creatures, the sun gods and fertility goddesses come to dominate, bringing with them the warmer seasons of year. March weather here in the Virginia mountains often reflects this epic battle, the starkness of winter lingering against the new growth of spring. At times, it truly feels like the clash of titans: strong winds, sudden snowstorms, rivers swollen with melted snow and heavy rains, and then the brilliant, warm days of spring that quickly help us forget the hardships of winter.

Coyote

Early in March, I see what looks like a large dog sitting on its haunches in the far field. Its fur is gray and bushy. After surveying the territory for a long time, the animal slowly meanders into the woods. That's when I realize it is a coyote. I am impressed with its calm confidence and the way it behaved as if it knew this place and spent time here often, though invisible to us.

We regularly hear coyotes. Their howling at night is legendary, sometimes a symphony of quavering yodeling sounds, sometimes a cacophony of high-pitched yipping—always awe-inspiring and a bit eerie. The hair rising on my neck hints at the primal fear our ancestors must have experienced when living with dangerous predators, such as wolves or mountain lions. I love hearing the coyotes from the safety of my house but would not want to encounter a pack while out alone in the woods.

Coyotes are adaptable to virtually all environments, from desert to mountaintop to urban setting. They are omnivores and eat rodents, rabbits, berries, and carrion. Here in the Highlands, farmers shoot coyotes on sight, as they will kill not only chickens and lambs, but also foals, calves, even pigs. According to the US

Department of Agriculture's Wildlife Services website, coyotes are responsible for over 60 percent of livestock losses to predators in the US, which amounted to 310,000 animals in 2020.[5] Coyotes are considered a nuisance species in Virginia. Despite local bounty systems and continuous open season for hunting and trapping coyotes, this animal has now spread to all counties in the state. Coyotes seem invincible; the more coyotes are killed, the more they adapt by producing larger litters.

All domesticated dog breeds are related to their wild cousin, the coyote. While house dogs are our mostly obedient companions, coyotes represent wild, untamed nature. Coyotes howl, hunt, roam freely, take what they need, and craftily resist being hunted to extinction. They are highly intelligent and use visual, auditory, olfactory, and tactile signals for communication. Coyotes remain wild but move into and through our human spaces to remind us of our own lost primal nature.

To many Native American tribes, coyote is known for his intelligence and cunning deceptiveness. Coyote characters vary widely across tribal folklore. Sometimes, coyote is a revered teacher and inspirational figure; at other times, he turns into a greedy and reckless villain who also chases females.[6] Very often, he is a loveable, funny trickster who applies reverse psychology to outsmart his opponents.[7] Whether appearing in animal or human form, he gets himself and others into constant trouble but always saves himself in the end with his cleverness. While Southwestern legends mostly describe coyote as a trickster, West Coast and Northwestern tribes consider coyote a transformer, creator, and benefactor who helped create the world, brought fire to the people, and taught other skills that advanced human civilization.[8]

Coyotes in their many impersonations capture the unpredictable March spirit, the dynamics between benevolent and life-giving spring energy and winter's reluctance to loosen its harsh grip.

The sighting of the coyote earlier this month was a strong nudge for me to get back outside, to smell, taste, and touch wildness again. When I opened the front door that morning, I took in deep, full breaths of crisp spring air. After buffering myself from the outdoors all winter, I am reclaiming my place in wild nature again.

March Garden & Landscape

By mid-March, I keep a bag of potting soil inside the house to warm it up to room temperature. I gather my seed flats from the garden shed and fill them with potting soil. After patting the soil in place, I draw grooves on the soil surface with my index finger, sprinkle seeds into the grooves, and smooth the soil before watering it.

Then I wait.

For the first three days, nothing visible happens. On day four, cracks appear where the soil has been lifted up by the seeds' underground expansion. Tiny telescopes pop out of the soil—broccoli and cabbage seeds are the first to sprout. Tomato and pepper seeds can take two weeks or longer to emerge.

I marvel at the mysterious life force compressed into these tiny seeds. A seed represents the womb of life; it breaks open when encouraged by moisture and darkness at the right time of year. I witness this miracle every single year and never take it for granted.

Outside, when I pass near the pussy willow on a sunny day, it sounds like a massive beehive. The bush is covered with a fluffy cloud of catkins dripping yellow pollen. The bees' first sugar rush of the season sets the stage for a mesmerizing symphony of swishing bee wings. The male pussy willow catkins provide the pollen our honeybees need to feed their larvae. Both male and female catkins produce nectar that nourishes bees and other insects.

Across the fields, the still-scarce green blades emerge from last year's brown thatch, at first a bit shy, like immigrants uncertain of their welcome here. But after several days of rain, large, fresh patches of green grass populate the landscape. In my garden, the cover crop of winter rye sowed late last year has turned into a juicy, jade-green carpet.

At the end of March, chives are the first cultivated herbs to grow in the garden; rhubarb's colorful red knobs are breaking through the dark soil, and garden sorrel puts out its first lemony-tasting leaves. The earliest spring flowers brighten the landscape with their sensual colors and fragrances: creamy white snowdrops, yellow and purple crocus, blue Siberian squill, yellow forsythia and daffodils, green and pink hellebores, and purple grape hyacinths.

Our woodlands are still barren, but I have already spotted my favorite spring ephemerals in the county south of us, at a lower elevation. Patience, they will awaken here soon.

FORAGED PLANT
Purple Dead Nettle (*Lamium purpureum*)

The earliest wild greens that can be foraged here in the Virginia mountains in late March include chickweed, purple dead nettle, henbit, and the very first dandelion leaves and flowers. I will highlight purple dead nettle, also called purple archangel. This invasive plant with its tiny orchid-like purple flowers is highly nutritious and packed with vitamins C, A, and K, and minerals in the form of iron, calcium, magnesium, manganese, and fiber. Medicinally, this weedy little plant contains antioxidant, immune-stimulating, antimicrobial, and anti-inflammatory properties, and helps reduce spring allergies due to its high levels of quercetin.[9,10]

While purple dead nettle with its square stem is a member of the mint family, it does not taste minty but rather grassy and deeply herbal. Its dry and highly textured leaves are not exactly a taste-bud-pleasing delight when eaten raw. However, the leaves, flowers, and stems can easily be incorporated into cooked dishes, made into pesto, blended into green smoothies, or simply simmered into a light-colored tea; add a small amount of honey to cut its astringency. This year, I am planning to make a dead nettle salve for itchy and inflamed skin,[11] a general first-aid medicine for my home apothecary.

After eating mostly carbohydrate-heavy cooked foods during the winter, my body craves lighter spring fare. The chlorophyll and vitamin-rich green smoothie I make from purple dead nettle and other early greens settles into my cells with a silent sigh of satisfaction. Finally, spring is here.

Spring Cleaning

An almost instinctual drive for spring cleaning possesses me. On the first sunny days, I wash loads of laundry and hang them up on the clothesline, a rite of spring. I wash winter scarves, gloves, hats, a few blankets. While it takes longer to hang my laundry on the clothesline than to throw them into the electric dryer, I enjoy handling each piece of clothing, attaching it with clothespins, and watching it flutter in the breeze. It's a working meditation that fills me with calmness and a simple *joie de vivre*. Dried by wind and sun, entirely free renewable energy sources, our clothes smell of spring flowers and sweet earth when I carry them back into the house at day's end.

In late March, seduced by a few warm days, I pull out the summer clothes I stored in suitcases during the winter, wash and dry them, and then place them in the closet and drawer spaces vacated by heavy winter clothes. Switching out winter garments for summer clothes is another spring ritual I look forward to with anticipation.

Inside the house, cobwebs need removing from the high ceilings. I vacuum up hundreds of Asian beetles that have been accumulating on windowsills and inside lampshades. Soon, they'll disappear magically from the house, only to be replaced by another invasive but short cycle of "slow" flies whose name I never bothered to learn.

Dan's version of spring cleaning focuses mostly on machines and chores outside the house: spreading a hundred tons of gravel on our quarter-mile driveway with his tractor, changing tires and spark plugs on his motorcycle, consulting his tractor repair manual to replace hydraulic fluid and air filter. More vehicle maintenance awaits as various machines and gadgets are pulled out of the garage where they have overwintered—rototiller, riding lawnmower, push lawnmower, and weed whacker.

Spring cleaning creates a fresh start as we release old, stagnant winter energy to clear space for the incoming spanking-clean spring energy.

Danielle Olson, in one of her *Gather Victoria* blog posts, describes the annual European ritual of creating a decorative, sacred broom:

"No spring cleaning could begin without the creation of the sacred broom, the besom. Not meant for everyday use, these hallowed tools were used to sweep out the old and sweep prosperity and happiness back in. Besoms were considered so powerful that making a wish when a new broom was first used would cause it to come true. Differing woods and branches like hawthorn, cherry, willow and ash (all with their own magical purposes) were used as a handle. Around this were bound reeds, grasses, broom, and long-stemmed herbs such as lavender, bay laurel, eucalyptus. Colored ribbons were often added for magical intent, green and yellow for abundance, pinks and red for love."[12]

I love the idea of crafting such a broom but never seem to find the time, as other spring cleaning activities keep me busy.

Magazine and social media articles on spring cleaning abound: spring cleaning isn't only about cleaning one's clothes and space but also decluttering one's life and mind. One such article suggests a *mental* spring cleaning through the practice of mindfulness, journaling, unplugging from the internet, and reconnecting with loved ones.[13] While it is enjoyable to read such articles, the actual work required to follow even a few of these suggestions can stretch over several seasons. Each year, I choose a different large project for spring cleaning. This month, I cleaned out my garden shed and found new homes for things I am ready to release from my life: an old scythe and other gardening tools we no longer use and buckets of clean play sand.

Parker Palmer, in an *On Being* essay, reminds us that spring is never just about daffodils and pussy willows. Before spring showers us with its beauty, there is a lot of muck and mud to contend with, a reminder not to allow ugliness to bring us down. The humble layer of good dirt needed for growing plants serves as a nudge to cultivate humility. Above all, spring reminds us that life and growth always return, no matter how harsh the preceding winter, no matter how challenging our life circumstances. Palmer quotes Camus: "In the midst of a seemingly endless winter, I discovered within myself an invincible spring."[14]

March Summary

This month's ping-pong exchanges between the starkness of winter and assertions of early spring can feel like an epic battle between two formidable opponents. The coyote trickster character personifies this back-and-forth between new incoming energies and well-established patterns. We want to burst out and grow along with spring's expansive life force, yet we are pulled back into old stagnant patterns. Ultimately, the irrepressible vital force wins.

Even our bodies demand a change from the calorie-rich foods of winter to the fresh greens and lighter foods of spring. Spring cleaning is a highly useful practice to sweep out lingering winter energies from our living space and our inner life. When we clear the cobwebs and push through the muck of life, we claim the air, sunshine, and nutrients needed for our unfolding.

Journaling Prompts for Self-Reflection

1. What are the energetic seeds (ideas/projects) you wish to plant this month?

2. What battles are playing out in your life? Are there any old, stubborn patterns and habits that need to be released? Do you sense any new energies wanting to come in?

3. What does your life look like when it is in balance? Imagine it, write it down, and/or create a vision board.

4. Where do you see coyote's trickster antics at work in your life? Who or what creates mischief, drama, and/or chaos? What is your response to this?

5. How does Camus's statement about the inner invincible spring resonate with you?

APRIL

Green

Dragonfly iridescence
Pine-scented forest green
Succulent emerald of newborn grass
Sparkling jade mountain streams
Mossy-moist pillows at the foot of spruce
Lime green willows
Spraying their graceful arcs
Avocado butter rich

Green is the Mother's breath
Her flowing hair
Her billowing garments
Green is the Mother's blood
Pulsating and undulating
Nourishing and smothering
Dying and birthing herself
Again and again.

Fertility, New Growth & Viriditas

My eyes inhale the color green, just as someone emerging parched from the desert would gulp down lifesaving water. My need for green may be as urgent as my need for water. In fact, the two are interrelated: without water, there would be very little, if any, green. Spring's fresh green vegetation feeds the cells in my body with its vibrancy. Green feels comforting, at once relaxing and energizing.

Perhaps the most intense and succulent green I've experienced grew in the rice terraces of Bali, Indonesia. The luminous color of the young rice seedlings was enthralling. An Indian reader of my Bali travel blog commented that the specific green color of the rice nursery plants is called *dhaani* in Hindi. She commented that "this color always seems to convey freshness, joy, and fecundity."

Hildegard von Bingen (1098–1179), a German Benedictine abbess, prolific writer, composer, and herbalist healer chose the word *viriditas* to capture the vitality and fecundity of new spring growth. *Viriditas* also came to describe spiritual and physical health. Hildegard's lifelong study and deeply intuitive understanding of the plants evolved into the European medicinal tradition called *Klosterheilkunde*, or monastic medicine.

Healthy Hildegard, a website dedicated to holistic health and wellness based on Hildegard von Bingen's teachings, explains that *viriditas* represents "the greening power of God," the life force that resides not only in the fertile landscapes outside of us but also needs to be cultivated inside of us, in our body and soul landscapes. We can internalize this divine green life force through the consumption of green plant food that keeps us energized and healthy and connects us with nature and the divine. Hildegard characterized life as a juggling act between the life-affirming qualities of *viriditas* and the vitality-robbing barrenness of *ariditas*. Physical disease and spiritual decay caused by insufficient green flow are examples of *ariditas*.[1]

Hildegard lived in the Rhine River Valley, near the town of Bingen in central Germany. The green, fertile environment of that region undoubtedly influenced her worldview and her teachings. I grew up in a similar environment in southern Germany, in the foothills rising from the Rhine River to the mountains of the Black Forest. Not surprisingly, I find myself living now in the Appalachian Mountains of Virginia, reminiscent of my native landscape.

In the mountains here, in April, fresh green grasses cover pastures and meadows. A soft lacy-green haze threads itself through the trees, bringing a quickening to the mountain landscape and vibrating the air all around. These shades of spring green offer deep satiety to eyes and souls starved for color all winter long. The brand-new green energy feels expansive and liberating. Anything seems possible at this time of year.

The cycle of new life has begun in the bird world as well. There are baby birds in the kestrel and bluebird boxes now. I hang up the hummingbird feeder on the porch, freshly washed and sterilized and filled with homemade sugar water. Within an hour, three males attack each other to gain exclusive access to the human-made *ersatz* nectar. While I am painting a barn quilt panel on the porch, I am thrilled to discover a rose-breasted grosbeak in the lilac bushes nearby. I cannot clean the paint off my hands in time to find the camera and take a picture of this rare visitor.

At the end of April, reliable as ever, I hear the first whippoor-will just after dark. Its call cannot be mistaken and really sounds like *whip-poor-will*, with a staccato-like emphasis on the first and last syllables. The whippoorwill chant revs up, gets faster and faster, then stops abruptly. A short while later the chant erupts from another location. Sometimes, it is so loud that I think the bird must be sitting on the front porch. When I have managed to open the door quietly, I have been rewarded with a brief glance of a dark bird on a nearby rock wall, just before it flies away. Despite their loud calls, whippoorwills are shy birds.

Eostre & Ostara

The pagan festival Ostara long preceded the Christian Easter holidays now observed during that same time period in late March to early April. Ostara was named after Eostre, a Germanic goddess of spring sometimes pictured with the shoulders and head of a hare. Little knowledge remains of Eostre. Her role as light bringer and goddess of the dawn who ensured fertility of fields, animals, and humans was all but wiped out by the Christian church.[2]

However, a few breadcrumbs of her existence remain. Saint Bede, a Medieval English monk and history scholar who lived in England during the eighth century, wrote a book on the origin of the names of the months. There he mentioned that April was named after a Germanic goddess, Eostre, in whose name spring feasts were celebrated. Over the centuries, many authors have questioned the veracity of Bede's writings while others, including Jacob Grimm, author of the 1835 book *Deutsche Mythologie*, have no doubt that Eostre existed.[3] Grimm wrote: "We Germans to this day call April *ostermonat* [Easter Month] ... This *Ostarâ*, like the [Anglo-Saxon] *Eástre*, must in heathen religion have denoted a higher being whose worship was so firmly rooted that the Christian teachers tolerated the name, and applied it to one of their own grandest anniversaries. ... *Ostara, Eástre* seems therefore to have been the divinity of the radiant dawn, of upspringing light, a spectacle that brings joy and blessing, whose meaning could be easily adapted by the resurrection-day of the Christian's God. *Bonfires* were lighted at Easter . . . Maidens clothed in white, who ... at Easter ... show themselves in clefts of the rock and on mountains, are suggestive of the ancient goddess."[4]

In the Christian world, Easter is still celebrated with colorful dyed eggs, chocolate bunnies, and new spring clothes, even by people who do not consider themselves religious. Have you ever wondered what Easter eggs and the Easter bunny have to do with Christ's resurrection, the religious focus of Easter?

According to anthropologist Krystal D'Costa, many ancient traditions view the egg as a symbol of rebirth. The egg also appears in creation mythologies. In ancient Egypt, the sun god was believed to have hatched from such a primeval egg. One of their main gods, Osiris, returned to life rising up from the shells of a broken egg. The legend of the Phoenix, a mythical bird, is similar. When its life was completed, it perished in flames and rose again in a new form from the egg it had laid.[5]

D'Costa writes that, in Hinduism, the act of creation itself occurs when the cosmic egg is shattered. The eggshells then become the heavens, the egg white turns into air, and the yolk forms the earth. In the Zoroastrian creation myth, the ongoing struggle between good and evil is represented by an egg-like universe pierced by the evil force. The Chinese have legends about a cosmic egg that gave birth to the first being. In Finland, Luonnotar, the daughter of Nature, accidentally breaks some giant eagle eggs. The pieces from these broken eggs then shape the world as we know it today: the sky and the earth are shaped from the shells, the egg yolks transform into the sun, and the egg whites convert into the moon.[6]

Thus, the egg has primordial significance. Long before eggs and bunnies were incorporated into Christian Easter celebrations, humans envisioned a cosmic egg that bears the seeds of the universe, earth, and her inhabitants. The egg holds all potential for life. It symbolizes the fertility of the earth and rebirth of nature. It is only appropriate, then, that eggs represent the beginning of life, as new growth is manifesting so forcefully in spring. The Easter bunny may just be a relic from the times of the goddess Eostre whose companion was the hare, a symbol of fertility.

Hare/Rabbit

Hares and rabbits belong to the same family (Leporidae), but they are different species, cousins rather than siblings. Hares are a bit larger and run faster than rabbits. They tend to be solitary while rabbits prefer large social groups.[7] For the purpose of discussing the mythological and folkloric symbolism of hare or rabbit, I treat them as interchangeable.

The hare is the companion animal of several European lunar goddesses including Hecate, Freyja, and Holda. As a nocturnal animal, the hare is associated with the moon, which rises in the evening and disappears in the morning. Both the moon and the hare were believed to die daily, only to be reborn at night, thus elevating the hare to a symbol of immortality. In many cultures, the hare is also a popular symbol of fertility, abundance, and rebirth. It is not difficult to see how, over centuries, Ostara's hare, a symbol of fertility, could have evolved into the Easter bunny who delivers eggs, symbols of rebirth, on the Christian holy day of resurrection.[8]

In African American folklore, Brer Rabbit is a trickster figure who originated from African folktales. Especially popular during slavery times, Brer Rabbit personified the weaker yet cunning animal who always managed to outmaneuver stronger, more powerful animals like foxes or wolves. Faced with slaveholders' efforts to eliminate any vestiges of African languages and cultures, enslaved people craftily used stories to keep parts of their culture alive and pass them on to their children. Folktales sometimes also contained coded information about secret meetings and escape routes.[9]

Similarly, the rabbit is a trickster animal among some southeastern and northeastern Native American tribes. For many Mexican and Central American tribes, rabbits are symbols of fertility, while Aztec legends associated rabbits with drunkenness and promiscuity.

Up close and in my gardens, our eastern cottontail rabbits can be destructive pests. One year, I had to build twenty small wire-mesh cages around my newly planted sweet potato seedlings because the resident rabbit really enjoyed their tender young leaves. When the rabbit could no longer access the sweet potato leaves, it decimated my beet seedlings. I was livid. Enough was enough! I set a trap with chopped carrot pieces inside. A few days later, the rabbit was my prisoner.

When I was a child, my father kept rabbits in a small hutch in the back of our house. We often pulled plantain and dandelion leaves from the yard and fed them through the wire doors but did not develop affectionate feelings for them. They were never pets, always just meat animals. Rabbit meat tastes good, similar to venison.

As I looked at my trapped rabbit, I was wondering what to do with it. My husband shook his head when I asked him whether he wanted rabbit stew for dinner. I didn't have the gumption to kill it myself. So, it was catch and release for this lucky rabbit. While it is technically illegal to relocate any wildlife, what choice did I have but to drive a considerable distance from home to release this one into the wilds? When I opened the cage, it cautiously hopped out, sniffed the air, then bolted away at lightning speed.

April Garden & Landscape

Warm, sunny April days can fool us into thinking that spring has taken up permanent residency. However, at our mountain elevations, warm days are often followed by multiple rounds of freezing nights or even a snowstorm. Hard frosts in the second half of the month make me fear for our peach and pear trees and the sour cherry bushes already bursting with blooms. All the other flowers—daffodils, tulips, hellebores, hyacinths, and even the young red shoots of peony—seem irrepressible. The grass continues to grow with determination as soon as the snow melts. I have noticed that the plants that are growing now have adapted to survive these temperature variations. It is the freezing nights during the month of May that can cause significant damage because less hardy plants are growing now and most trees have leafed out by then. May freezes often destroy the fruit harvest for the year and leave behind foliage that appears burnt. Some years, there are no apples in the entire county except in small protected corners aptly named "Little Egypt" or "Banana Belt."

The woodlands on our property are finally beginning to adorn themselves with spring ephemerals: dainty purple-and-white hepatica, subtle spring beauty with her pink stamens, creamy white bloodroot (the name hints at the dramatic red color of her root), and trout lilies dangling yellow bells above speckled tulip-like leaves. Across the state, Virginia bluebells cover entire woodland areas with their sky-blue blossoms, creating magical fairyland groves and often attracting throngs of visitors during peak bloom. Golden ragwort colonies are Mother Nature's treasure flung generously across wooded hillsides. Pawpaw trees are opening their dark maroon flowers; strange to think that such a small flower can produce our largest native fruit. When I spot purple dwarf larkspur along backwoods roads, I feel richly blessed to be living here.

Gardening already takes its toll on my body. Repetitive motions from squeezing small and large garden clippers and pulling weeds with deep root systems take much physical energy and often lead to tenderness and pain, especially at the beginning of gardening season. I schedule weekly massages to ease my lower back and wrist pain.

Pain or no pain, I am determined to remove the young vetch already growing around my raspberry bushes. I had so admired the deep purple flowers when they first showed up along the orchard fence and allowed them to go to seed. That was a big mistake. During the following years, vetch vines climbed exuberantly up my raspberry bushes and anything else they could use as a ladder to expand vertically. My raspberry harvest was noticeably diminished because of this invasive intruder.

Sometimes, there's an upside to the tedious work of weeding. I discovered one of the electronic dog collars that had gone missing. I don't know how it ended up inside a wire cage protecting the trunk of an apple tree. Perhaps the dog dug underneath the cage and yanked off the collar when he pulled his head back out? Maybe the dog was attracted to the scent of a chipmunk or another small animal that burrowed around the tree roots. Some mysteries remain unresolved.

Early in April, I find small amounts of apple mint, miner's lettuce, yellow rocket (known as creasy greens in Appalachia) with flower buds similar to broccolini, and wild onion chives. Later in the month, I make flower syrups from forsythia, magnolia, and violet petals, which I gathered hastily the day before a predicted frost. Pulling some greens here, finding some edible blossoms there, and gathering a few flowers into a bouquet for the table while meandering around my property are some of my favorite spring activities.

The ancient forager soul in me rejoices in the abundance of wild food and medicine now available: chickweed, dead nettle, stinging nettle, garlic mustard, ramps, creasy greens, miner's lettuce, dandelion, violets, and redbud flowers. In my foraging classes, I witness a transformation in my students as they learn to identify, harvest, and prepare wild food. Many are deeply moved by their experience as they discover a long-lost relationship with the wild plants around them.

FORAGED PLANT
Common Chickweed (*Stellaria media*)

Common chickweed is my favorite wild spring food. Its leaves create moist hillocks dotted with tiny white flowers whose star shape led to the Latin name *Stellaria*. It prefers shady places, such as the woodland edge behind our shed, but will spread in large mats in the garden, on lawns, and in waste areas. Once the sun gains strength later in spring, chickweed grows gangly and begins to dry up. However, it remains juicy and green for another month or so in protected shady areas.

Chickweed greens have a mild, slightly sweet taste and are packed with vitamin C, beta carotene, and minerals, including iron, calcium, magnesium, and manganese. Because of its high iron content, it is often incorporated into herbal blood-building formulas. I enjoy making sparkly green smoothies and delicious pesto with chickweed and sprinkling it raw on salads and omelets.

Chickweed's soothing medicinal properties can bring down inflammation and histamine reactions, regulate kidney function, reduce triglyceride and LDL cholesterol levels, and heal burns and insect bites. Taken internally, chickweed tincture helps ease a dry cough, bronchitis, and asthma. It also reduces joint pain and helps heal mouth sores, sore throat, and hemorrhoids. As a gentle laxative, it can ease constipation and other digestive issues.[10]

Applied externally, chickweed tincture is antibacterial and can be used to cleanse wounds. As a poultice, it reduces itchy inflamed skin from insect bites, rashes, eczema, and burns. I love to make a soothing chickweed salve for minor skin infections and irritations.[11]

It is important to correctly identify common chickweed: individual plants are six to ten inches tall. Their smooth, oval leaves have a pointed tip and grow paired along the stem. A line of tiny hairs that spirals around the main stem is best viewed by holding the plant up against the light. The flower has five white petals, but they are so deeply divided in the middle that it looks like there are ten. There are several other types of chickweed, for example, mouse-ear and star chickweed, with hairy leaves that are not nearly as tasty as common chickweed. Most importantly, beware of scarlet pimpernel, a poisonous look-alike with a square smooth stem and a similar leaf arrangement. Once pimpernel's peach-colored flowers appear, it cannot be confused with chickweed anymore.

Foraging Wild Green Superfoods

Continuing with April's green theme and Hildegard of Bingen's teachings on the divine green power of plants, let's take a deeper look at what modern science knows about chlorophyll. Green plants manufacture their food through photosynthesis, a process using the pigment chlorophyll, which gives plants their green color. Chlorophyll has one main function: to absorb sunlight and transfer it to energy-storing molecules in the plant. The stored energy converts carbon dioxide and water into glucose, an essential nutrient that helps the plant to grow. This process of photosynthesis releases oxygen into the air, essential for most other life forms, including our own.[12]

Plants, algae, and certain bacteria all use their chlorophyll pigments to harness energy from sunlight to produce oxygen and glucose. Herbivores nourish themselves by eating plants, and carnivores get their energy from eating herbivores. Humans, whether herbivores or omnivores, depend on the plants' photosynthesis for energy and the ability to grow and repair tissue and bone. We are sustained by the oxygenated air released by plants. Essential to all types of ecosystems, chlorophyll is the foundation of life on our planet.[13]

Chlorophyll = green = life on earth.

Almost one thousand years ago, Hildegard of Bingen was right after all.

Wild greens rich in chlorophyll meet our body's need to transition from heavier winter fare to lighter spring foods. Their impressive nutrient value and abundant availability make them first-choice greens, free for the picking. Also, spending time outside foraging wild plants provides physical activity and exposure to sunshine that boosts our vitamin D production. Wild greens are a delightful addition to almost any meal, and their varied flavors wake up our taste buds: tart, peppery, lemony, or sweet.

Wild greens and "weeds" are nutritional powerhouses, true superfoods when compared with both conventionally and organically grown garden crops. In addition to chlorophyll, wild plants provide rich sources of vitamins, minerals, and healthy fats like omega-3 fatty acids that are difficult to procure from store-bought plant food.

The humble dandelion, sadly considered the bane of many a lawn owner, offers up all of its parts—leaves, buds, flowers, stalks, and roots—for our nourishment. According to a US Department of Agriculture analysis, raw dandelion greens contain an impressive amount of nutrients that include A, B-6, C, and K vitamins, calcium, folate, iron, potassium, magnesium, phosphorus, beta carotene, lutein, and trace amounts of zinc, copper, manganese, selenium, thiamin, niacin, and riboflavin.[14] When compared with nutrient values of popular greens, such as spinach, kale, and Swiss chard on the same USDA site, dandelion leaves offer higher levels of iron, vitamins A and E, beta carotene, phosphorus, and lutein. In addition to exceptional nutritional values, dandelion also provides the following medicinal benefits: it stimulates liver and digestive functions, strengthens bones, and cleanses the blood. Dandelion can relieve skin problems like eczema, diminish inflammation and swelling, and repopulate healthy gut flora;[15] in short, it provides an entire medicine chest full of helpful remedies.

Europeans value dandelions and other wild greens as essential ingredients for prized dishes such as cream of dandelion soup in France, nettle broth and dumplings in German and Scandinavian countries, and pasta with wild fennel and mustard leaves in Italy. Similarly, Greek cuisine makes ample use of *horta*, a general term for fresh or cooked wild greens.[16]

Our modern produce is grown in increasingly depleted soils, often artificially fertilized and sprayed with herbicides and pesticides that diminish its nutritive value while poisoning us with remnants of these chemicals. Even organically grown produce often has less nutritional value than foraged wild greens, the original unadulterated plants from which our modern produce has been hybridized during ten thousand years of agriculture.

Jo Robinson, in her book *Eating on the Wild Side*, traces our modern produce varieties back to their ancestral versions and examines the changes in nutrient levels that have occurred since then. From the beginnings of agriculture, farmers chose to cultivate plants that were high in starch, sugar, and oil, sacrificing vitamins, minerals, fiber, and antioxidants in the process. Some of the earliest cultivated plants were figs and dates, very high in sugar, and starchy grains that provided large amounts of carbohydrates and calories per serving. Plants with high fat contents, such as olives and sesame seeds, were also selected preferentially for early cultivation.[17] Robinson observes that "for the first time in our long history on the planet, we humans no longer had to eat bitter or fibrous food or spend hours every day processing our food to make it fit to eat. We were creating the food supply of our dreams."[18] Unfortunately, improvements in taste achieved by breeding out sour, astringent, or bitter-tasting compounds led to a loss in vital phytonutrients that protect us against disease.

Robinson mentions sweet corn as an example of an extreme deviation from its original version. Teosinte, the ancestral corn that grew in the Americas, originally contained 30 percent protein and only 2 percent sugar. In a stunning reversal, today's sweet corn contains up to 40 percent sugar and only 4 percent protein. While people may believe that eating sweet corn is a healthy "vegetable" choice, there is actually little difference between eating a chocolate bar, pita bread, or sweet corn. All of them raise our glycemic index to a similar level.[19]

The glycemic index is a ranking of the degree to which foods increase our blood sugar levels. Most vegetables and fruits have a low glycemic index (<15 to 50), and grains are in the intermediate range (55–70). Eating many low-glycemic foods, only moderate amounts of intermediate-glycemic foods, and very few high-glycemic foods helps us lower our risk of cancer, heart disease, chronic inflammation, obesity, and type 2 diabetes.[20] However, according to the Centers for Disease Control, only 10 percent of Americans eat the recommended daily servings of fruit and vegetables necessary for a low-glycemic diet.[21]

We need a diet rich in high-nutrient foods to be healthy. Wild greens such as dandelion, winter cress, purple dead nettle, and chickweed are undoubtedly among the most nutrient-dense foods we can consume. Even city dwellers can find these plants in parks, riverbanks, or empty lots.

In her book *The Wilderness Cure*, Monica "Mo" Wilde, a Scottish herbalist and forager, wrote about her year of consuming only foraged wild foods. During that year, she noticed profound changes in her health. Inspired by her own experience, Wilde created a study to explore the effects of eating wild foods on the human gut microbiome. She enlisted twenty-four participants who ate only wild foraged foods for either one month or three months. These two cohorts were compared to a group of twenty-four people who ate only store-bought foods.

The study called The Wildbiome Project was sponsored by the ZOE Health project, founded by Professor Tim Spector, a gut microbiome researcher at Imperial College London. The tests used in this study assessed microbiome composition and key health parameters of people eating an exclusively wild food diet. Findings reported by Wilde were as follows:

Two-thirds of participants improved their cholesterol and triglyceride levels. Vitamin D and iron levels improved, while magnesium, vitamin B12, and other key nutrient levels remained constant. Inflammation levels dropped, despite the consumption of wild meat and fish.

Overall, there was an improvement in HbA1C, a blood marker of diabetes. One participant with diabetes returned to a prediabetic state within two weeks of eating wild food. Participants also saw improvements in hormonal balance, sleep, and happiness. In addition, all overweight participants lost weight, and all improved their BMI and waist-to-height ratios, even those who had found losing weight hard to do when eating conventional foods.[22]

Wilde's findings confirm what my body already knew: wild foods are indeed beneficial for our health and may help us reverse some of the health problems caused by an industrial food diet.

Many of the maligned invasive plants, such as garlic mustard, autumn olive berries, and kudzu, are edible, medicinal, or beneficial in other ways.[23] We can make use of the edible or medicinal parts of these undesirable plants before destroying them to support the growth of more beneficial native plants. Garlic mustard, which was introduced to the US in the early 1800s as a food crop, has spread abundantly into many different environments, including deeply shaded woodlands. This wily plant secures and expands its living space by releasing a chemical compound into the soil that slows the growth of nearby plants, even trees. Garlic mustard and other invasive plants choke off native plants. Douglas Tallamy's work on the importance of native plants as food sources for native wildlife has become seminal within a growing native plant movement.[24] Native oak trees, for example, are hosts to over four hundred caterpillars and native wildflowers, such as goldenrods, support more than one hundred species of caterpillars and native bees. In contrast, non-native invasive autumn olive trees support only fourteen species of wildlife. Without habitats that provide sufficient nutrition, insect and butterfly populations diminish and consequently lead to drastic decreases in the bird population. The US has lost nearly three billion songbirds since 1970, according to the Cornell Lab of Ornithology. One of their key recommendations to rebuild essential wildlife habitat is to reduce America's sixty-three million acres of lawn by planting native species.

One of my own action steps to support the growth of native species includes turning autumn olive berries into a nutritious juice or jelly before cutting down the trees, and harvesting garlic mustard greens for dinner while also tearing out as many plants as I can reach before they go to seed. In this manner, I make use of their nutritional benefits while also diminishing their presence on our property to allow more native plants and wildlife to reemerge.

I feel lucky to be surrounded by dozens of wild foods as soon as I step off my porch. In a walk around my house this month, I jotted down forty wild edible plants. Many more plants will grow during summer and fall. I much prefer to pull some chickweed, cleavers, dead nettle, violet, and dandelion leaves for my green smoothie than pay money at the store for a green "superfood" powder that comes in a plastic container that later ends up in the landfill. Wild greens are free, loaded with phytonutrients, need no packaging, and require only minimal labor to harvest and enjoy them.

April Summary

April vibrates and bustles with the life force in its many manifestations. By celebrating spring with the symbols of rabbits and eggs, we are connecting to ancient times when the egg held all potential for life and the hare symbolized the fertility of the land and the eternal cycle of nature. Hildegard's *viriditas* captures the vitality and fecundity of spring. She basically told us a thousand years ago to "eat your greens" so we can benefit from this green life force that keeps us healthy physically and spiritually. April's expansive green energy invites a renewed embrace of life and all its offerings.

We owe our very lives to the plants that not only generate the oxygen we breathe but also provide high-quality nutrition. This month demonstrates clearly how plants, animals, and humans are intimately connected, something our ancestors recognized and celebrated. Can we embrace this interconnection once again and let it enrich and expand our existence?

Journaling Prompts for Self-Reflection

1. What feelings or sensations does the color green evoke for you? What is greening in your life right now?

2. What are you most looking forward to in spring?

3. What symbolizes new beginnings for you?

4. What sparks new ideas for you?

5. What brings renewed vitality into your body and soul?

MAY

Full Moon

Luna Silver Moon,

She who swells
oceans into frothy frenzy
then calms them
with a lullaby.

She who cajoles
seeds deep in soil
to sprout green telescopes
into the unknown above.

She who summons
the adventurer and the dreamer
across the seas, across the skies
to new lands and new lives.

She who speaks a
language so ancient,
few translators
are left alive.

Luna Silver Moon,

Tonight, you imprint your perfect fullness,
and sweet, insistent light
into the farthest corner of my
ancestral memory.

Exuberant Fertility, Sacred Marriage

May brings warmer weather and a sense of freedom, expansion, and exuberance. As the mountainsides wrap themselves completely in shades of green, the valleys grow luminous spring grass and vast patches of wildflowers. The life force is accelerating into a full sprint. One afternoon, as I am driving with my windows down, jazz music wafting from the car stereo, I drink in large gulps of the beauty all around me. How deliriously lucky I feel to be part of this place dotted with sheep and cows, trees, fence lines, and hills shaped like immense loaves of bread.

Was I floating in a beautiful dream? Has anyone ever gone mad with beauty? Beauty so boisterous in its serenity that I forget the social disagreements, political divisions, and other malignancies dominating the news. The roadside wildflowers, sounds of birds, wind, water, and the ever-changing light are elements that absorb humans and livestock into themselves without their essence being changed. I want to share this gobsmacked beauty with the world and pass out parcels of its tranquility to others so they, too, may experience it.

But even if I could send serenity in a bottle, not everyone would be transformed by it, and if too many arrived here, they'd somehow manage to disturb and alter this place to fit their wants and needs. Beauty interrupted, stolen, co-opted, harnessed. That's what humans do: we dig here, fell trees there, smooth the wildness into tame comfortable spaces for ourselves.

Just not on this day; this day is perfection.

A robin couple begins construction of their nest under our porch roof. I'm a bit worried when I see them weaving their little home with dried grasses. Two semi-feral cats claim the porch as their God-given territory. While they have learned to ignore the hummingbirds mobbing the feeder, they will not ignore the robin fledglings when they eventually leave their nest and practice their hopping and flying skills. I remember the year when robins had their nest in the lilac bush nearby and a black snake ate one of their babies, forcing the others into premature flight. Maybe our porch will be a safer place after all?

Barn swallows inspect the porch rafters. Last year, one couple built a nest above our entry door. They deposited wet white splotches right in front of the threshold, poop I had to scrub away every single morning. Luckily, this couple seems interested in the spot above the light fixture under the overhang, far enough from the door. I can deal with swallow poop at the edge of the porch. Mosquito control in exchange for poop cleanup. The swallows chitter and fly aerial acrobatics over our heads while we sip our morning coffee on the porch.

Beltane & the Green Man

Early May is the midpoint between the spring equinox and the summer solstice. May Eve (the eve of the first day of May) was celebrated as Beltane by the Celts, Walpurgisnacht by the Germanic tribes, and Floralia by the Romans. This was a time to wear green to honor the arrival of spring and also a time of sexual freedom. The Maypole, center of village festivities, represented the god's phallus implanted in the womb of the earth.[1] In his form as a foliage-covered man with leaves and vines growing out of mouth and ears, the Green Man has similarly been interpreted as the male principle of creation. Many medieval cathedrals in Central Europe display the Green Man as architectural decoration.[2]

Beltane celebrates the peak of spring, when the life force is bursting into fullness through the sexuality and fertility of the earth and her inhabitants. The maiden goddess, Flora, also called Goddess of Spring or the May Queen, falls in love with the Young Oak King, Jack-in-the-Green, or the Green Man. After consummating their love, the May Queen becomes pregnant. Flora and Jack have entered the Sacred Marriage, the archetypal union of earth and sky.[3]

In the United Kingdom, festive parades still mark Beltane. A particularly vibrant celebration occurs in Hastings each year. The streets are filled with men and women in green costumes who greet Jack-in-the-Green, the Green Man, with song, dance, and general merriment. I recently learned that Greenbelt, Maryland, in suburban Washington, DC, also organizes an annual Green Man festival.

I have been intrigued by the Green Man, wondering about his origin and whether other cultures had similar mythological characters. It appears that he may have popped up in many places around the world. Over five thousand years ago, the ancient Sumerians spoke of Humbaba, the guardian of the cedar forest. Pashupati, the horned Lord of the Beasts, first appeared around 3000 BCE in India. Seated cross-legged in a yogic posture, surrounded by animals, he is worshipped as an incarnation of the Hindu god Shiva. Egyptians, Phrygians (ancient Turkey), Tibetans, and Aztecs all honored a similar male nature deity.

Islamic Sufism mentions a revered man called *Al-Khidr* (The Green One or The Verdant One) who appears spontaneously and imparts wisdom and mystical knowledge. Al-Khidr could be seen as a mediator between the divine realm and the physical world.[4] He came in many incarnations throughout history and may have taken the role of Khadir, servant to Alexander the Great. The two of them searched for the well of life, rumored to hold the secret of immortality. As the two men entered a cave in the mountains of the Sahara desert, Khadir fell into a well and obtained immortal status. Alexander, on the other hand, died at age thirty-two.[5]

Neo-Pagans and Wiccans consider the Green Man a version of the horned god, who in turn may be a derivation of several earlier nature and fertility gods. A possible forerunner of the Green Man may include Faunus, an ancient Roman forest spirit known for his unrestrained primal male sexuality. Faunus has been depicted as a human male with horns or as a human-goat hybrid creature. He did not possess human language and communicated only through the sounds of nature. Both men and women invoked him when seeking to cure infertility.[6]

Another predecessor could have been Cernunnos, the Celtic horned god. He was the ruler of the natural world and bestowed wealth on those who deserved it. He appeared in a man's body crowned with stag antlers.[7] Engraved on a silver bowl dating back to 30 BCE, an antlered Cernunnos was seated in a cross-legged position surrounded by animals, similar to the Indian god Pashupati.[8]

Even though the horned god was turned into the devil by the Christian church, he nonetheless found his way into Christian symbology as a divine messenger in the form of a stag. According to legend, the aristocrat Hubertus went deer hunting on horseback sometime in the seventh century. Suddenly, an enormous white stag appeared to him with a shining Christian cross suspended between his antlers. When Hubertus kneeled down in front of the apparition, the stag admonished him to live a godly life and to adopt ethical hunting practices. Hubertus converted to Christianity and was later sainted. Saint Hubert has become the patron saint of the hunt. This story appears on the website of the American company that distributes the German herbal liquor Jägermeister (master of the hunt). The official label on the Jägermeister bottle still bears the image of the stag's head with a cross between his antlers,[9,10] the horned god and the Green Man in disguise persisting into modern times.

In Basque country in northern Spain, the Basajaun is the lord of the forest who guards the flocks of sheep at night. Often depicted as a large, hairy, human-like figure, he sometimes also wears antlers on his head.[11]

In the Caribbean, Papa Bois or Gran Bois is known as the protector of the animals and the forest. He is pictured either as a physically powerful old man or as a human-animal creature with cloven hoof and horns. Papa Bois is revered as a major deity in the voodoo religion. He commands healing powers and possesses the secrets of life and death. Possibly of Congolese origin, he may have become fused with a Taino (Native Caribbean) deity, who was incorporated into the voodoo pantheon.[12] Papa

Bois is a mysterious figure who still appears in contemporary Caribbean art and folklore.

In Ecuador, Sacha Runa ("forest being") has become the symbol for people and organizations wanting to preserve the Amazon rainforest. Sacha Runa protects animals and instructs shamans in their plant work. His female counterpart is Sacha Huarmi, Green Woman or Jungle Woman. She and Sacha Runa are intermediaries between humans and plant spirits.[13]

Given that the Green Man has appeared in so many different locations, time periods, and cultures, I choose to think of him as a primal male archetype, a part of our collective unconscious, a trace of our ancestral memory, when we were still an inherent part of nature, not outside of it, not above it. The Green Man seems to predate the arrival of the patriarchal gods who wielded authoritarian hierarchy and violent domination. He appears to represent a healthier male principle much needed as a complement to the feminine principle of divinity.

Hummingbird

There are over 330 species of hummingbirds, found only in the Americas and nowhere else in the world. The hummingbird (*Trochilidae*) family includes some of the most exotic-looking birds I never knew existed with names such as green violetear, long-tailed sylph, booted racket-tail, spangled coquette, and rufous sabrewing. Can you imagine a punk-rock bird with a red mohawk, another one with a beak longer than its body, and one with white cotton balls around its feet? Always, the males are the most flamboyant, as if some painter designed them under the influence of a hallucinatory drug.

Here in Virginia, we have only one representative from the Trochilidae family: the ruby-throated hummingbird. Its iridescent colors are derived, not from pigment in the feathers but from prism-like cells in the feather structure. This is why the male's throat color, also called the gorget, can appear black, red, or orange depending on head position and light reflection. When the light hits just right, his throat feathers flash the most brilliant red, then turn black with a mere turn of his head.

You hear hummingbirds before you see them. They sound like large droning insects with their wings flapping up to two hundred times per second. Hummingbirds have a ball-and-socket joint in their wing that allows them to fly backward and upside down. In slow motion, you can see their wings perform a figure-eight pattern instead of an up-and-down motion. Male hummingbirds are fiercely territorial and dive-bomb each other brutally, sometimes stabbing each other in the belly with their long dagger beak. When they attack, they hiss, whistle, and screech, cutting through the air like missiles. To court and impress a female, the male performs a semicircular dance accompanied by a sound I can only describe as a short burst of a World War II fighter airplane in kamikaze mode.

Because of their rapid metabolism, hummers must consume more than their body weight in nectar in one hour. A bird weighing three grams has to consume close to four grams every hour, which amounts to over forty grams a day, the equivalent of sipping one thousand to two thousand flowers. Flower nectar provides electrolytes, protein, and calories and supplies three times the amount of calories of the sugar water in the feeder.[14]

Please do not buy the red-colored commercial sugar solution. The homemade version, while not as nutritious as flower nectar, is healthier for the birds and easy to make: one part sugar to three parts water, heated to dissolve the sugar, then cooled. Replace this solution frequently, especially during hot days when it can easily begin to ferment.

Since hummingbirds exist only in the Americas, hummingbird legends are primarily found among Native American and Central American people. Many Native American tribes associate this tiny bird with good luck and other positive attributes, such as healing, beauty, and harmony. There are hummingbird clans and hummingbird totems, especially among Northwest coastal tribes but also among the Pueblo in the Southwest. In ancient Mexico, the hummingbird was the divine companion of the Aztec god Huitzilopochtli. The god himself was sometimes artistically depicted in the form of a hummingbird.[15]

To me, hummingbirds bring joy and beauty but often surprise with their tenacity and fierceness. They are always welcome in my gardens as important pollinators and delightful entertainers.

May Garden & Landscape

Everything is growing now with determination and fervor. In the flower garden, lupines stand straight and tall with their purplish-blue blossom spikes. Sky-blue irises release a subtle floral perfume. The peony buds appear more pregnant each day and will soon shake open their frilly petal skirts. Knapweed offers its blue and purple flowers as a mandala prayer to the sun. The dog rose unfolds its first white blooms, and locust trees are drooping with intensely fragrant white blossoms. Comfrey has spread itself around my compost pile, and I approach it slowly to avoid spooking insects and being stung. Its dangling purple blossoms attract all sorts of interesting pollinators.

Native plants in the landscape and woodlands include camass lilies, wood poppies, wild geranium, trilliums, and columbine. Finding rare plants like wild hyacinths and native orchids, such as pink and yellow lady's slippers, always evokes adoration and protective instincts in me.

Our orchard trees and berry bushes have developed tiny baby fruit full of promise for an abundant harvest later in the season.

Every morning, I move houseplants and seed flats out onto the porch and bring them back in at night to give them a chance to get used to temperature fluctuations and to withstand sun and wind, hardening off for their outside life. Dan tilled the garden for me so I can plant peas, onions, potatoes, broccoli and cabbage seedlings, and sprinkle lettuce and radish seeds into the dark soil. I harvest asparagus every other day, a thick handful of stalks destined for our breakfast omelets. Strawberry plants are beginning to bear small green fruit, and I can see the robins eyeing them for the first tinges of red.

In its essence, gardening is about planting seeds and maintaining conditions for them to grow into their full potential. This requires soil preparation, mulching with compost, and weeding. Exuberant seedlings only want one thing: to root themselves in the soil and sprout as tall and as wide as their genetic blueprint will allow. Soil is the living, crumbly substance that is womb to most of our real food. The more I learn, the more I am in awe of the deep, moist mysteries the soil holds.

We pick up two trailer loads of old manure from a nearby horse farm during our yearly visit with the owners. They have mountains of sheep and horse poop in various stages of decomposition and are happy to get rid of as much as we care to take. I enjoy chatting with the wife while Dan exchanges views and news with the husband. This year, I bring them an armful of rhubarb, a fistful of chive blossoms, spring greens, and peach jam from last year, in return for the stuff that makes it grow so well by enriching our soil. We also pick up a trailer load of cast-off growing soil from a mushroom farm. I use it as mulch around my seedlings, as it still offers nutrients to my plants along with moisture protection and weed suppression. Recycling someone else's waste into another productive application is a win-win situation in a circular practice that puts resources to use in multiple ways while minimizing waste.

FORAGED PLANT
Stinging Nettle (*Urtica dioica*)

Foraged foods are abundant this month and include blue violets for jelly, stinging nettle for mineral-rich teas and asparagus-nettle soup, locust blossoms for fragrant tea and fritters sweetened with maple syrup, lamb's-quarter for mild greens and pesto, dandelion leaves as a refreshing bitter green, and dandelion blossoms for jelly and wine. I am choosing to highlight stinging nettle here for its many beneficial properties.

I grew stinging nettle from seed to bring it onto my property. It now happily spreads itself in our front field. Why would I deliberately introduce a plant that burns my skin if I am not careful? Its sharp hairs contain formic acid and histamine, which can lead to irritated and blistering skin.

I planted stinging nettles because they offer so many gifts in the form of food, medicine, fiber, dye, hair rinse, and soil conditioner. Stinging nettles are deeply nourishing and healing, as they contain an impressive amount of phytonutrients including vitamin K, beta carotene, calcium, boron, copper, iron, flavonoids, protein, and so much more—a total of 183 chemical constituents.[16] Nettles' high mineral content strengthens hair, teeth, skin, and bones. They also contain natural antihistamines that help alleviate allergies. They detoxify all body systems; build blood; support kidney, adrenal, and thyroid functions; and strengthen our body's response to environmental pollutants and molds. Nettles can also reduce blood sugar levels in diabetics and calm arthritic joint pain.[17,18]

I enjoy making a dark green tea from nettle leaves. It has a complex flavor that feels deeply nourishing to the body. I often dehydrate young nettle leaves to add a handful to soups or other dishes later. Once the leaves are dried or cooked, they no longer sting. Still, when I touch the dried leaves, my skin has a faint, anticipatory reaction, as if remembering the last time I was stung.

Nettles can be cooked like spinach. I love blending it into a deep-green thick paste as a side to grains or a dip for fritters. Nettles can be infused into oil and turned into a salve or ointment. They make a nutritious base for a salad dressing when infused in vinegar, the best medium to extract their mineral content. Nettles are useful as a natural green dye and can even be used as a hair rinse. Nettle fibers are so sturdy that they can be turned into clothing, rope, and fishing nets.

While stinging nettles are safe for most people, they can produce side effects for a few including stomach problems and diarrhea, urinary issues, sweating, hives, or rashes. Stinging nettles may also interact with certain drugs such as blood thinners and medications for heart disease, diabetes, and high blood pressure.

Gardening as Therapy & Resistance

Beyond the basics of providing food and medicine, gardening is an act of resistance for me. By growing my own food using organic and permaculture practices, I bypass the industrial food system, refusing to purchase its denatured, chemical-laden food products. By growing my own food I am rebelling against commercial agriculture and Big Pharma, both enormous industries more concerned about their profits than my health.

By growing my own food, I resist being a pawn in the modern consumer culture that encourages consumption not just as a necessity but also as entertainment, as distraction and the implicit lure of filling an empty inner space of which most people are only vaguely aware. Modern consumer culture alienates us from the production of our food, both the hard labor and the intense gratification. All we need to do is hand over some paper money or a plastic card, and we receive a bag of food in return. For the most part, we don't know where it comes from, who grew it, and what the true environmental, political, and socio-cultural costs of this purchased food are.

By growing my own food, I resist outdated beliefs that farming involves only manual labor requiring brawn but little brain; beliefs that devalue the quintessential activities that produce the food that keeps us alive; beliefs that miss the complexity of knowledge required to grow food from seed, nurture it, harvest it, and transport or process it before it reaches and nourishes us.

As the child of blue-collar workers seeking to escape my parents' life, I internalized the classist thinking that manual labor is inferior to intellectual or white-collar work. I was the first person in my family to pursue higher education and obtain a doctorate.

I proved that I possessed ample brainpower, but, over the years, I realized that intellectual work was not necessarily more rewarding or intrinsically more valuable than physical labor. I need both to feel whole, and I can see how each cross-pollinates the other.

Working with the soil is *not* a brainless activity or menial work. Growing things ensures our health and survival and requires a wide array of physical, intellectual, and relational skills. As the bumper sticker on a car proclaimed: "No Farms, No Food."

Growing my own food makes me more tolerant of the diversity of shapes and textures in produce, beyond the uniform size and unblemished appearance of produce displayed on supermarket shelves. All produce from my garden finds its use, one way or the other, to prevent food waste. If beans spent too much time on the vine and have become stringy, or squashes grew too large and coarse when hidden under leaves, they become incorporated into the food I prepare for our dogs, along with grass-fed organ meats, castoffs from a nearby farm.

Growing my own food makes me aware of the vagaries of weather, how dependent we truly are on nature for our food— how drought, fire, cold or heat, disease or pests can diminish or eliminate an entire season's harvest. It is humbling and necessary to know this firsthand.

Beyond resistance to forces I do not want to support, I embrace values of self-reliance through practicing and teaching valuable skills that have been sidelined due to ever-expanding urbanization and over-reliance on machines and specialty businesses.

I also welcome the "earth gym" opportunities that my work in the garden provides—physical activities that help my body stay in shape and provide sun exposure for vitamin D production.

My garden is my place of therapy, my sanctuary. When I pass through the garden gate, I leave the outside world behind. I enter Zen mode, a state of flow. My time awareness slips away as I move from one activity to another, until, hours later, I notice the low angle of the sun, my body's weariness, and my need for food and rest.

In the garden, I continuously learn about the interplay of the forces necessary to sustain life. And I soak up many spiritual lessons from the plants, consciously and unconsciously, lessons about patience, slowing down, coexistence, abundance, joy, loss, renewal, trust, and surrender.

May Summary

May is possibly my favorite month of the year, full of exuberance and joyful hummingbird action, the life force in accelerating mode. Researching the Green Man in his many different manifestations led to several personal insights: while the Green Man sometimes does not possess human language, he does communicate through the sounds of nature, the swishing of leaves and grasses, the creaking of branches, the snorting of deer, the rustling of a beetle on the ground. These sounds are such a rich language—if we can transcend the narrow definition of our own human language consisting mostly of words. We can train our ears to listen to these sounds when we go outside, away from car noises and the pinging of our phones. The Green Man also has helped me look beyond the toxic masculinity of patriarchal systems, and offers hope for healthier masculine energies to, once again, take root and complement the life-giving and nurturing feminine principle.

In May, gardening moves into full swing, as I plant seeds and seedlings and marvel at their transformation into the food and medicine that sustain our own bodies. Gardening helps me reclaim my intimate connection with food and supports healthy movement and often a contemplative state of mind that turns the garden into a microcosm for important life lessons.

Journaling Prompts for Self-Reflection

1. How important is it for you to experience beauty? Where do you find beauty in your world?

2. We often refer to Nature as Mother Earth, as female. How does it feel to introduce the male principle in the form of the Green Man? What aspects of Nature do you experience as female, which ones as male? A Navajo (Diné) friend introduced me to the concept of "male" and "female" rain. How would you imagine these different types of rain?

3. How do male and female principles show up in your life, within yourself?

4. What plants attract you? What plants do you stay away from? Why?

JUNE

---

*Refuge in the Peace of Wild Things**

There is a place inside of me
    that opens wide
    into meadows of grass and flower
    that grows tall to caress
    the stony face of mountain
    that snakes quietly
    down the currents of river.

There is a place inside of me
    that falls wide awake
    with the scratchy cawing of raven
    the plaintive moan of cow
    the serenade of cicada
    and a sudden rush of wind
    through the treetops.

There is a place inside of me
    that sweeps down the valley with wind
    tussling butterfly wings here
    crashing fiercely through trees there
    as I listen hard for anything
    wind might fling my way.

*Title inspired by Wendell Berry's poem "The Peace of Wild Things."

Wildness & Domestication

June is filled to the brim with exponential growth of plant life and
abundant animal fertility in the form of baby birds, white-spotted

fawns, fur-ball groundhogs, fluffy rabbits, and playful bear cubs. I have always found the juxtaposition of wildness and tameness in nature striking, how baby plants and young animals appear so tame and cuddly before they mature and become ferocious and wild in the pursuit of survival.

I wonder what forms of wildness remain in us humans, beneath our domesticated ways of being. Not the scary, out-of-control, and violent behaviors that cause terror, chaos, injury, and death. Instead, I am curious about a different kind of wildness: the part in us that knows without question that it belongs to an all-encompassing nature, that opens sensory tentacles and accesses knowledge directly from the wind or a tree and taps into the vast reservoir of our ancestral ways of being.

Some years ago, we raised ducks and geese inside a fenced area that housed a tiny inflatable swimming pool and a wooden pen for shelter. Every few days, the fence, pool, pen, and birds had to be moved to a new patch of fresh grass because the old area had become dirty and depleted. As soon as we replaced the pool water, the birds refreshed themselves and promptly soiled it again. Tired of changing their water daily, we fenced off a nearby small pond for them. For the first time in their lives, our ducks and geese were able to swim in a real pond.

Nothing prepared us for the wild and joyous scene that unfolded: these birds swam and dived and lifted their wings; they stuck their heads underwater searching for invisible food at the pond bottom and picked on the grasses growing at the water's edge. The water was in constant rippling motion as the six of them swam in circles. Muddy brown water pearled off their white feathers. They frolicked all day and left the water only after sunset to settle in their pen for the night. The pond was theirs now. Their innate nature as waterfowl required it.

This experience made me think more deeply about our own innate wild nature. Diane Ackerman described our life between birth and death as "a savage and beautiful country."[1] That is the wild life I am referring to. Following my own wild nature includes my ability to take risks and engage in adventures, to have a meaningful impact without tamping down my own true being, and to continue my lifelong learning about the many subjects I deeply care about. My own wild life also includes experiencing myself as part of nature and reclaiming some of the instincts and skills we have lost over the course of many centuries. The body/mind split that values mental facilities over physical functions was introduced into European cosmology and exported during colonial times to most corners of the world. More recently, urban living and technology have disconnected and alienated us even further from our deep nature connection.

Ecopsychologist Dr. Michael J. Cohen has identified fifty-four senses and sensitivities that we have either lost entirely or no longer use consciously. These include radiation senses (light, sight, temperature), feeling senses (proximity, gravity, motion), chemical senses (pheromones, moisture sensitivity), navigation sense, and many others.[2] How would our human experience of nature expand more fully if we learned to access even a few of these lost senses? Would some of these senses help us reclaim our innate wildness?

When our wild nature remains undeveloped, we shrink into the tameness of scripted living. Like ducks out of water, we still manage to waddle around and do what we need to do to stay alive. But when we express our authentic, creative selves, the heart rejoices, the blood pulses faster, the body dances, the cells sing. We become a living prayer, a thanksgiving to the divine nature that stirs in us and demands to unfold.

Flora & the Oak King, Summer Solstice

Flora was the Roman goddess of flowers and vegetation who bestowed fertility on the earth, animals, and humans. When people wished for prosperity and abundance, they petitioned Flora. She has been portrayed as a beautiful young woman crowned with flowers.[3] While her Floralia festival was tradition-ally observed from the end of April into the beginning of May, I take the liberty to claim Flora's energy for June here. Spring arrives later in the Virginia Highlands than it does in the Piedmont and coastal areas of the state. I feel Flora's energy strongly now, as the landscape comes fully alive with blooming trees, shrubs, and wildflowers scenting the air with intoxicating perfumes.

The Roman poet Ovid (43 BCE–7 CE) wrote that Flora started her life as a nymph who blossomed into a fertility goddess after Zephyr, the god of the west wind, kissed her.

Flora may have originated from an earlier Mediterranean fertility goddess. But when she was known as Flora (derived from the Latin word for flower, *floris*), she was one of the four-teen most important deities in the Roman Empire. The Romans built two temples in her honor. Julius Caesar even turned the Floralia period into an official holiday, not just a one-day affair but an entire week of public revelry that included games, theater plays, and circus entertainment. At times, the dancing and revel-ing escalated into public nudity and open sexual activity. Roman authorities attempted to reign in these wild excesses by prohibit-ing nudity. Eventually, by the fourth century, all pagan festivals were outlawed under Christian rule.[4,5]

Such strong energy emanates from the flower world. I honor Flora's energy when I bring flower bouquets into the house, cap-turing a bit of her magic to adorn and scent my home. Some people claim that every flower has its own flower fairy, also called devas. Could flower fairies be Flora's bountiful offspring, her flower chil-dren spread around the world by her husband, the wind god?

Summer Solstice: In the northern hemisphere, the summer solstice on June 21 is the defining day of the month and the offi-cial beginning of summer. It is the longest day of the year. The full moon around this midsummer period is called the Honey Moon for the mead that was prepared with honey and enjoyed freely during solstice celebrations. Mead was treasured as a divine bev-erage representing the life-giving properties of the sun.

Our ancestors believed that the sun came to a standstill on the solstice, which spanned the three days of midsummer, and then began its return journey. Their fervent hope that the sun would remember its path across the sky gave rise to solstice myths and celebrations around the world.

Celtic celebrations of Midsummer Eve honored the Oak King and his symbol, the mighty oak. As fire represented the sun and the Oak King at their peak, massive bonfires were lit and kept blazing through the night until sunrise the next morning. People danced joyously around the fires and playfully jumped through the flames. The Oak King, whose reign began six months earlier at the winter solstice, is now in his prime. From midsummer onward, however, his power begins to wane as the sun loses its ferocity.[6]

Similar to the Oak King, other sun deities associated with solstice celebrations included Balder and Mithra. Balder, the Norse god of light, and Mithra, the Persian god of light, were both born on the winter solstice, and their strength culminated at the summer solstice. The brilliant light from Balder's throne radiated out to all corners of the world. But Balder died during the summer solstice. His death was always followed by rebirth six months later, symbolizing the eternal life-death-rebirth cycles marked by the solstices.[7] Mithra, in his role as the god of light, created plants and animals and the movement of the celestial bodies.[8]

One year, around summer solstice, I attended a nature retreat in the Blue Ridge Mountains. We were instructed to hike to the top of a mountain and wait for the sun. Rising in the dark, we began the steep climb up the mountain. When we arrived at the top, we each found a place to sit and waited.

I could hear the wind whistle through the valley below us and saw a small animal scampering through the underbrush and a hawk gliding by at eye level. Gradually, daylight increased, but the sun would not show itself, even though there were few clouds in the sky. As I sat there on a patch of moss, wrapped in a blanket, I wondered, "What if the sun refused to rise today, or ever again?

How would our world change?" An anxious tension spread in my belly, as I felt how our ancestors might have experienced this uncertain time before sunrise. I imagined them asking the same questions and understood why they felt the need for ritual and prayer to bring the sun back from its nighttime wanderings. Finally, the first sliver of sun sent rays of golden light across the mountain ridges, gradually chasing away the deep shadows on the hillsides.

Ah, the sun: it did rise after all! We were safe once again from darkness and certain ruin. I felt such unexpected joy, assured that everything would be all right, at least for that day. From this mystical experience, I caught a glimpse of the primal significance of the sun and the solstices in the lives of our ancestors. The sun defined their lives, their crops, their fertility, and their abundance—or the lack thereof. This is true for us modern humans too; we just don't know it in the same way our ancestors did.

Mountain Lion

Mountain lion is my personal symbol of sheer and utter wildness; no other animal in my current environment comes even close.

Mountain lions occupy large territories across the Americas, from the Yukon in Canada to Tierra del Fuego in Argentina. Their superpower is their adaptability to vastly different environments. They thrive in dry deserts, forested mountain ridges, and tropical jungles. Once found throughout the United States, they are now mostly limited to the western states and Florida. Heavy bounty hunting in the early 1900s and ongoing persecution in response to livestock killings, along with habitat loss and fragmentation have severely decreased the mountain lion population. They are called by different names depending on location: puma, cougar, catamount, or panther. I will use mountain lion here.

Mountain lions are among the fastest and most powerful animals, capable of killing large prey with their teeth and claws. They are agile and strong, able to jump as high as eighteen feet, quickly scale a steep cliff, or leap a distance of forty feet. While they can take down large mammals such as elk and deer, they can also subsist on smaller animals like rabbits, mice, and even insects.

According to the Mountain Lion Foundation, these animals are both keystone and umbrella species and play an essential role in preserving healthy ecosystems and biodiversity: "While a *keystone species* is a species on which other species in an ecosystem largely depend, such that if it were removed the ecosystem would change drastically, an *umbrella species* is a species that has either large habitat needs or other requirements whose conservation results in many other species being conserved at the ecosystem or landscape level."[9]

The Virginia Department of Wildlife Resources has declared the eastern cougar extinct while acknowledging 121 "unconfirmed sightings" in twenty-nine counties in Virginia.[10] My own close encounter left no doubt that they are here.

I was walking down our gravel road to the mailbox. Close to the main road, I saw movement in my peripheral vision. A mountain lion had just wandered around a rocky outcrop and was now in full view. We both stood very still, staring at each other with surprise and suspicion, a mere twenty yards separating us.

All my senses on high alert, body frozen, I was keenly aware that I had no weapon of any kind, no walking stick, no pepper spray, no handgun—just my bare hands. What would I do if it attacked me? Neither one of us moved in that long eternity of time expanded by fear.

I kept staring at the animal, thoughts tumbling through my mind: *Is this real? Am I in danger? Will I end up being this big cat's lunch?* Somehow, I remembered to check the length of its tail so no one could later tell me that I had seen a bobcat instead. No doubt, this was a mountain lion!

Finally, the creature averted its gaze, turned around, and slowly walked back into the tall beige grasses behind the rocky outcrop. And here was the second surprise: it immediately disappeared out of view, perfectly camouflaged, creating no visible movement in the grass. It was gone, leaving no trace except for the breath that slowly seeped back into my lungs.

While I can now claim that I stared down an apex predator, this encounter radically transformed my sense of security and ownership of my land. Gone were the times of innocent ambling across the fields and through the forest without at least carrying a bear spray canister on me. This was still wild territory. However, instead of feeling terror, I felt a stirring inside of me, something coming more fully alive, as if the mountain lion had gifted me with some of its power.

At the time of this encounter, I was writing a manuscript about an abusive experience in a cultish group. Staring down this mountain lion was not so different from standing up to that group's authoritarian leader whose spirit animal happened to be mountain lion. Mountain lion helped me locate her fierce independence within myself as I deprogrammed from the cult's influence and reclaimed my personal power. With mountain lion fierceness, I knew that I would never again turn over my power to anyone else. Time to rewild myself!

Mountain lion infuses tribal lore throughout the Americas. Many Native American tribes revere the mountain lion as a sacred animal (Shoshone, Hopi) or protector of their tribe (Hopi, Pueblo, Zuni, Mohave, Navajo). The Apache consider mountain lion a harbinger of death, an evil omen connected to witchcraft. The Quechua People in South America, on the other hand, believe that puma is a positive omen promising good fortune and wealth. For the Incas of the Andes, mountain lion was the loyal companion of Viracocha, the creator of the universe.[11,12]

June Garden & Landscape

The monumental increase in biomass during the month of June always amazes me. At first, seedlings seem to linger while they establish their root systems. Then, seemingly overnight, leaf production goes exponential and quickly covers the brown soil in between the seedlings. Onions and potatoes are thriving. Garlic is ready for harvesting. I will tie about eight plants together into small bundles and hang them up under the porch rafters to fully dry. Tomato bushes are establishing themselves, while corn plants and summer and winter squashes are still tiny. But lettuces, radishes, and other cooler-weather greens are flourishing now. In the flower gardens, poppies, peonies, larkspur, elderberry, daisies, and roses all compete for pollinator attention and our visual and olfactory appreciation.

Viper's bugloss, oxeye daisies, golden alexanders, campion, goat's beard, Bowman's root, Solomon's seal, Virginia spiderwort, multiflora rose, wild honeysuckle, purple vetch, black walnuts setting fruit, wild cherry trees with green, pea-sized berries, mountain laurel splendid in their pink blossoms, mass plantings of blanket flower and coreopsis along a new stretch of highway, Indian cucumber root, pink lady's slippers, purple spikes of lupines, and red- and yellow-rimmed native columbines, comfrey blossoms buzzing with insects. Everywhere I turn, nature is in full expression of her life force.

FORAGED PLANT

Lamb's-quarter (*Chenopodium album*)

Lamb's-quarter, also called wild spinach, is growing abundantly now as "weeds" in my garden. Even as it is getting too hot for other spring greens, such as lettuces and garden spinach, lamb's-quarter thrives. Wild spinach is highly nutritious and has far more fiber, beta-carotene, vitamin C, riboflavin, calcium, zinc, copper, and manganese than regular garden spinach.[13]

I love whipping up green smoothies that are a blend of lamb's-quarter greens, berries, lemon juice, and maple syrup, a refreshing, chlorophyll-rich vitamin shot. I often incorporate the chopped leaves of lamb's-quarter into omelets and stir fries. I also make a delectable green sauce by cooking the leaves and thin stalks with onions, salt, pepper, and nutmeg, then blending it into a smooth emerald béchamel. Later in the season, I dehydrate leaves and seeds and grind them into nutritious flour. Mixed with wheat flour, lamb's-quarter flour adds a unique green color to baked products such as crackers, rolls, or breads. The dried leaves have a slight salty flavor that makes a subtle seasoning for any savory dish. Seeds can be sprouted as microgreens, adding live nutrition even to winter meals. As a cousin to quinoa, its seeds smell just like quinoa grains, a bit nutty, intriguing, nutrient rich. Whatever I use it for, lamb's-quarter always adds a wild food touch to our menu.

In addition to exceptional nutritional qualities, lamb's-quarter also provides medicinal benefits: the chewed leaves make a soothing poultice for insect bites, sunburn, minor cuts, and arthritic joints. As a tea, it reduces internal inflammation, settles stomach aches, and builds blood with its high iron content. Tea from its leaves also serves as a cleansing body wash, doubles as a refreshing mouthwash, and tames bad breath. The roots contain saponins, which can be used in soapmaking.[14]

Lamb's-quarter thrives around the world, wherever humans have gardened and disturbed soil. It is in the Amaranthaceae, or amaranth, family, which also includes garden spinach, Swiss chard, beets, and quinoa. In Africa, Asia, and Australia, it is commonly used as a cooking green.[15]

It is important to learn the difference between lamb's-quarter and similar-looking toxic nightshade varieties. Hairy nightshade (in the *Solanum* family), for example, can mimic the shape of lamb's-quarter leaves. However, nightshade does not have the powdery substance found on lamb's-quarter. Also, nightshade flowers are noticeably different. Their white petals with yellow center clearly distinguish them from lamb's-quarter's tiny green flowers shaped like a miniature broccolini wand.[16]

Rewilding Ourselves

What exactly *is* rewilding? And how do we begin to rewild our environments and ourselves?

Environmental rewilding aims to restore an area to its natural, uncultivated state by reintroducing native plants and wildlife. Such efforts can be on a small scale, by planting native wildflowers in a backyard or seeding a field with native flowers and grasses, or on a much larger scale, such as introducing wolves or elk to a designated wilderness area. Successful environmental rewilding can help counteract climate change and species extinction. Groups and organizations that promote environmental rewilding and conservation include the Rewilding Institute, the Nature Conservancy, and the Rainforest Alliance.

Humans who managed to avoid modern civilization have been labeled *primitive* and *savage*. The last five hundred years of mostly European colonization of all continents and internal expansion in countries where nomadic tribes existed (e.g., China, Japan, Scandinavia, parts of Africa) have resulted in the virtual extinction of "wild" people. The few remaining hunter-gatherer societies (Inuits, San Bushmen, Saami) survive in habitats that cannot be brought under agricultural cultivation, where climate conditions are so extreme that most other people cannot survive there.[17]

Anthropologist Hugh Brody, who has spent many decades living with various hunter-gatherer groups, observed that these cultures are very different from the stereotypes we have placed on them. They are often egalitarian and nonhierarchical, and they possess finely honed technologies that keep them in balance with their environment, climate, and local flora and fauna. Mental illness and addictions are extremely rare.[18]

What can we learn from these hunter-gatherer cultures? Even as most of us now live in urbanized areas, we *can* rewild ourselves by learning skills and activities that help us reclaim a more natural and less domesticated state of being. This also requires examining our cultural conditioning and undoing unhealthy modern practices.

A quick internet search yields many classes that teach basic wilderness survival skills, including fire making, tanning animal hides, and creating cordage from plants, but also techniques to help novices become more comfortable with spending time in nature and foraging for wild foods. Rewilding can take many forms, and each person decides to what degree they want to pursue it, making it achievable even for city dwellers. Two intriguing books allow us to follow the authors' sincere commitment to rewilding themselves in the modern world: Mo Wilde wrote *The Wilderness Cure: Ancient Wisdom in a Modern World*, describing an entire year of eating only wild foraged foods from sea and land while living in the United Kingdom.[19] Jessica Carew Kraft wrote *Why We Need to Be Wild: One Woman's Quest for Ancient Human Answers to 21st Century Problems*. She introduces us to her teachers and describes not only what Stone Age survival skills she learned from them, but also how her personal and social lives were affected, all within the larger context of cultural, historic, legal, and economic ramifications of such rewilding attempts in the United States.[20]

Brianne DelaCruz describes rewilding as a way of reconnecting with nature and discovering a more holistic and authentic way of life. Exposing ourselves to the natural elements of earth, air, wind, water, and fire helps us feel more grounded and alive. The benefits of unearthing our wilder selves include expanded creativity, greater access to our instincts, a better understanding of how to nourish body and soul, and knowledge of how to become better stewards to the land and ecosystems surrounding us.[21]

DelaCruz's suggestions for rewilding ourselves include spending both brief and extended periods in nature, engaging in nature-related activities such as keeping a nature journal, learning to identify the plants and wildlife in our environment, and foraging for wild foods. She also adds activities to reconnect us with our body through physical movement and observing seasonal markers such as solstices and equinoxes. She reminds us of the pleasure derived from bringing nature indoors by decorating our homes with natural materials such as stone, clay, and natural textiles. Another important aspect of rewilding ourselves includes unplugging from the digital world whenever possible.[22]

I would add the following to this list: learning not only the edible but also the medicinal benefits of plants. The medicinal use of plants helps us deepen our connection to plants and can become an important part of our self and health care. In addition to interior decorating with natural materials, we can clothe ourselves with natural fabrics such as linen, cotton, wool, and silk. Walk or bike as much as possible and slow down to the pace of nature, even if only for a weekend or a half hour after work.

Even one of these nature reconnection activities can get us started; we don't have to practice them all. You can choose one activity, allow yourself to be drawn in deeply, and notice where it takes you and what it will lead to next. DelaCruz reminds us that rewilding is a lifelong process.

June Summary

The summer solstice and full-throttle expansion of plant and animal life this month and a mountain lion encounter invite reflection on our domesticated existence and what's left of our inner wildness. Given the loss of so many of our ancestral senses, skills, and practices, how do we reclaim a connection with nature? Where do we start to rewild ourselves, and what does it look like for each one of us in light of our unique life circumstances, resources, and personal abilities? June is a great month to examine our cultural conditioning in preparation for letting go of any unhealthy modern practice we no longer want to support. You are encouraged to create your own definition of rewilding and to consider what a more authentic, nature-connected way of life would look like for you personally. The writing prompts below can serve as a starting point.

Journaling Prompts for Self-Reflection

1. What does your inner wild nature look like? If you aren't sure, have you ever caught a glimmer of it?

2. How would you live if you fully expressed your innate wild nature? How would it differ from where and how you live now?

3. Have you had a close encounter with a wild animal? What was your experience?

4. Which one(s) of the lost senses mentioned in the chapter made you curious? How would you pursue learning more about it; how would you reclaim it?

5. Which rewilding activity mentioned in the chapter are you most drawn to? How would you pursue this activity?

JULY

Fairy Dance

At sunset,
the fairies dress
in orange satin and
crimson silk
to honor the sun goddess
who colors their cheeks
with her fading breath.

Swaying coyly,
they flare their hems
and scent the air
with longing
and danger.

Intensity, Summer Heat & Outdoor Life

By July, many household activities have moved to our covered front porch, which bears witness to the work that happens there: muddied shoes tucked under the bench, sweaty clothes hung over the railing, herbs spread out on newspaper for drying, garlic and onion bundles dangling from the rafters to cure before they move inside for winter storage. The porch is a transition place. Vegetables, fruits, herbs, and flowers from the garden and the land get sorted and cleaned before they come into the house. The porch also serves as a summer kitchen, especially for the hot and laborious work of canning. I can fruit jams, chutneys, and tomato sauce on a camp stove to avoid generating additional heat from the kitchen stove inside the house.

The porch is a place to receive friends and other visitors, the perfect place to socialize informally. Sometimes surprise guests drop by: a grasshopper, a praying mantis, colorful moths resting on the siding of the house after slamming themselves against illuminated windows and screens, bugs of every shade and form, hummingbirds, swallows, and house wrens favoring the rafters as a place to build their nest. On my porch, the world is whole and thriving. The porch is its own ecosystem that reminds me to maintain balance in my life: work, pleasure, health, exertion, rest, beauty, peacefulness, and conversation that deepens and slides into sublime stillness.

I love July for its opulence; its audacious display of lushness; the vivid orange, red, and yellow of summer blooms that thrive in the heat of the sun; the sheer biomass of everything coming into its fullness. July is June's wildness on steroids.

"Everything is blooming most recklessly; if it were voices instead of colors, there would be an unbelievable shrieking into the heart of the night." (Rainer Maria Rilke)[1]

Summer's over-the-top expansiveness and exuberance can become manic and then exhausting and depleting. The heat and humidity, the dryness of soil when rain and thunderstorms bypass us, the fatigue and headaches from too much sun exposure. On hot days, I find myself irritable and listless; everything requires extra energy and effort. After spending time in the garden during the cool morning hours, I retreat inside as the sun rises in the sky, and my creative energies go dormant for the day.

Sun Gods

The sun was honored as a primal life-sustaining force by many cultures. In her book *A Dictionary of Nature Myths*, Tamra Andrews observes that "people across the globe from the most ancient of times recognized the power of the sun as provider, creator, and sustainer of life. . . . an all-powerful god . . . [who] upheld the order of the universe and guaranteed not only his own resurrection but also the resurrection of the earth."[2]

The Babylonian sun god Shamash traveled across the sky from the Mountain of Sunrise to the Mountain of Sunset, then withdrew for the night to feast with his wife.[3] The Greek sun god Helios rode across the sky in his chariot, leaving behind his eastern palace every morning, resting in his western palace for the evening. During the night, he sailed across the river Oceanus back to his eastern palace, where his journey began all over again the next morning.[4]

In Middle Eastern and Asian cultures, sun gods were seen as omniscient judges who prevailed over the human world. Hindus had Mitra, who helped guard against evil and brought light to the world. Mithra, the Persian god of light and heat, was the all-knowing judge of the living and the deceased.[5]

In Inca Peru, ancient Japan, and ancient Egypt, sun deities had additional functions as the ancestors of the royal family.[6] Perhaps the most enduring sun god celebration is the Inti Raymi, the annual Peruvian Festival of the Sun which has been celebrated since the mid-1400s. Inti Raymi is observed during the southern hemisphere's winter solstice (concurrent with the June summer solstice in the northern hemisphere). Incan architectural structures were built to mark the position of the sun at the solstices. On the day of the solstice, the elders, priests, and other elite members of the Incan empire gathered at dawn to greet Sun God Inti as he rose over the mountains. In worshipping Inti, they also asked for a good harvest. It was Inti who provided the light and warmth for agricultural crops and livestock to thrive.[7]

Spanish colonizers banned this festival as a pagan ceremony, though it continued to be observed secretly for centuries. Since the 1940s, the festival has become very popular again and attracts thousands of tourists. Inti Raymi is now officially part of the Cultural Heritage of Peru.[8]

Wild Turkey

Wild turkey mamas lead their babies across our property on a regular basis this month. We see them foraging in a large group on most days. As summer progresses, the number of young turkeys in these bands gradually diminishes, most likely due to predation.

Turkeys, indigenous to the Americas, are related to grouse, pheasants, and other fowl, including the domesticated chicken. In North America, there are two species of wild turkey: the eastern wild turkey (with five subspecies) and the ocellated wild turkey of the Yucatan in Mexico. Wild turkeys were domesticated by ancestral Pueblo people in the Southwest region of the United States and by the Mayans in Mexico at least two thousand years ago.[9,10] Once near extinction, wild turkeys can now be found throughout the continental United States. The eastern wild turkey has made an impressive comeback through restoration programs and is the most prolific subspecies throughout the eastern half of the United States and into Canada.

Unlike domesticated turkeys, which are densely crowded into long turkey houses and kept almost immobile while being fattened for slaughter, the wild turkey in its natural habitat is a majestic bird. Wild males sport a "beard" on their chest, a set of modified bristle-like feathers that can grow up to seven inches in length. The blue coloring of their heads and the bright pink-red wattle dangling from the chin are striking; the sharp spurs on their legs are dangerous weapons in a territorial fight with a competitor. Females have a more modest, mostly brown coloration and have neither beard nor spurs.[11] It is interesting to read the descriptions of these wild birds when shot by hunters during turkey season: they always state the weight of the bird and the length of his beard. Appendage length seems to matter greatly.

Wild male turkeys are quite a bit larger than female hens. Males are called gobblers, after the "gobble" call they use to attract females. Only male turkeys make this particular sound; females cluck and chirp to communicate.[12]

A hen typically lays a clutch of ten to twelve eggs over a period of about two weeks. She then incubates her eggs for almost a month.[13] In our area, baby turkeys (poults) hatch in June and, by July, follow their mamas across the fields as they learn to forage for food. Two adult females will often band together, one leading the group, the other heading up the rear, watching for any sign of predators. This large, blended family group covers roughly the same terrain each day, slowly roaming across the grassy meadows looking for tasty snacks. When the hens sense danger, they alert their babies, who hide or fly away into the nearest tree. Turkeys can run at speeds of up to twenty-five miles per hour and fly as fast as fifty-five miles per hour.[14] It always surprises me when I see one of these large, heavy adult birds become airborne. In fact, turkeys sleep in trees every night as protection against ground predators like coyotes, foxes, raccoons, and bobcats.

By about six months of age, males from the same brood break away and form a sibling group that stays together for life and defends the group against outsiders.[15]

Their omnivorous diet includes grasses, berries, seeds, acorns, insects, and even small snakes and salamanders. I unwittingly learned about a specific food source for wild turkeys. After researching planting strategies for ginseng and determining the perfect forest site, I carefully spread six pounds of expensive ginseng seeds on the raked forest floor and covered the seeds loosely with leaf litter. The following years, I returned to that site expecting to see ginseng growing but never found a single plant. While watching a band of turkeys roaming through that area, it finally dawned on me that every one of my precious ginseng seeds had become turkey food.

Turkeys were highly prized in ancient Mayan culture, and their images are frequently found in archaeological ruins. The Mayan empire stretched from southern Mexico throughout Central America. Because their local ocellated turkey with its cherished multicolored feathers could not be tamed, Mayan elites in Central America had turkeys imported from Mexico, where they had been domesticated as early as 300 BCE. Mayans venerated turkeys as godlike figures and symbols of power and prestige. Turkeys were sacrificed during New Year celebrations to usher in fertility and abundance.[16]

In the United States, Native Americans honor the turkey as the bringer of agriculture and a symbol of fertility. An Apache legend speaks of turkey bringing corn kernels to humans and instructing them on how to plant corn, thus sparking the beginnings of agriculture. Starting over two thousand years ago, turkeys were used for ceremonial purposes in the Four Corners region, likely to ensure fertility at the time of spring planting. Turkey feathers stabilized arrows and were incorporated into the ceremonial clothing of many tribes.[17]

Anthropologist and archaeologist Cyler Conrad reports that ancestral Pueblo peoples in the Southwestern region of the US carved long turkey bones into flutes or whittled them into tools such as awls, beads, and tubes. They also wove turkey feathers into warm blankets. Egg white was used to blend paint pigments. Representations of turkeys including their tracks as stylized designs frequently appear in ancient rock art and on ceramic fragments found in that region.[18]

In the world of animal symbology, turkey is a symbol of fertility and abundance and a reminder to practice gratitude for what we receive.[19] Not surprisingly, a roasted turkey has become the centerpiece of today's Thanksgiving feast in the US.

July Garden & Landscape

The garden is in full production this month. I am harvesting onions, potatoes, the first cherry tomatoes, and peas, which thrive in the cooler summer weather here in the mountains. A second sowing of lettuces, radishes, green beans, and peas is in the ground. Corn stands almost chest-high, and winter squashes spread their massive leaves between the corn stalks blooming and setting fruit by the end of July. Pole beans are beginning to curl up around the corn stalks. I always plant the Three Sisters, a Native American companion planting method that combines squash, beans, and corn in the same patch.

The orange blossoms of scarlet runner beans dot the green leafy curtain that wraps itself around the bamboo teepee poles and creates a secret place inside, the perfect hideaway for a child or a rabbit.

Soon the hyacinth beans will open their voluptuous purple blossoms, and loofah vines will erupt into a profusion of little yellow flowers. The cucumbers are also beginning to climb up on their trellises, eager to explore vertical space. Along the garden fence, mulberries, blueberries, currants, and sour cherries are ripening and provide prolific fruit, mostly for the birds who often get to them before I do. The thickets along the forest edge offer raspberries and blackberries.

The flower garden has expanded into its summer fullness, with stands of blood-red bee balm and lavender wild bergamot, creamy yarrow, orange calendula, cosmos and jewelweed, purple phlox, magenta echinacea, black-eyed Susans, and sky-blue bachelor's buttons—a feast for the eyes and pollinator haven for many insects, including the mysterious clear-wing hummingbird moth.

We work outside in the morning and in the evening, avoiding the hottest part of the day. We check daily for ticks, and treat poison ivy outbreaks, mosquito and other insect bites, scrapes and bruises—the inevitable sequelae of time spent outside. In the evening, we settle on the porch after dinner, exhausted from the demands of the day but deeply content.

FORAGED PLANT
Wild Bergamot (*Monarda fistulosa*)

Wild bergamot, also called Oswego tea, purple bee balm, or wild oregano, is a striking native wildflower. Each of its many lavender blooms mimics a miniature fireworks explosion. Dozens of flowers in a colony create a spectacular focal point. Wild bergamot is easily recognizable along roadsides, where it grows up to three feet tall, but it is almost twice as tall in rich garden soil. Beyond its visual attractiveness to the human eye, I enjoy watching the different insects, butterflies, moths, and hummingbirds sipping its prolific nectar and surrounding the plant with humming sounds and vibrant aliveness.

I was delighted to discover several wild bergamot colonies on our property and brought this wildflower into my flower gardens to enjoy its presence up close. In the garden, it blooms for at least two months, beginning in July. Like other members of the mint family, it spreads through underground rhizomes. I see new colonies pop up in surprising locations, far away from the initial planting.

Wild bergamot has both culinary and medicinal uses. Its leaves and flowers are edible though spicy-tasting, similar to oregano, and can easily overpower a dish or a tea. The dried flowers look beautiful in a tea blend or sprinkled on salads. I like to mix wild bergamot leaves and flowers with peppermint and sweeten the tea with honey. I have also added a few handfuls of the leaves to meat dishes that needed some culinary excitement.

Wild bergamot is not the source of the essential oil used to flavor Earl Grey tea. That flavoring is derived from a citrus fruit called bergamot orange (*Citrus bergamia*) and is not related at all to the wild bergamot plant discussed here.

Wild bergamot was well-known to Native Americans, who valued this plant for its medicinal and cosmetic applications.[20] It is also one of the aromatic herbs used in sweat lodges for its calming and centering qualities.[21] Wild bergamot's medicinal properties are astonishingly diverse, as it contains antioxidant, anti-inflammatory, antibacterial, and antifungal constituents. Teas, tinctures, facial steams, infused oils, and compresses can be prepared to address a variety of ailments ranging from headaches, insomnia, colds and fevers, heart trouble, skin rashes, burns, and urinary tract infections, to intestinal worms and colic in infants.[22,23] Wild bergamot has especially high levels of thymol and geraniol, antiseptic compounds that are effective in a mouth-wash for combating bad breath and preventing tooth decay.[24]

There are more than twenty plant species in the *Monarda* family, which also includes red bee balm, horsemint, and lemon bergamot. Their flavors vary, and their medicinal applications overlap, so they are not interchangeable and need to be researched separately.[25] I have come across only two contraindications for wild bergamot: do not use during pregnancy, and be aware that it may aggravate existing heartburn.[26]

Injuries, Insect Bites & Other Maladies

Living and working in these wild Virginia mountains has resulted in many more physical injuries than I ever experienced in our previous suburban lifestyle. Thankfully, nature generously offers plant treatments for most of these injuries and mishaps. I harvest many of my home apothecary medicines during the month of July. These include yarrow, mullein, wild bergamot, calendula, English plantain, echinacea, jewelweed, elderflowers, red clover, St. John's wort, heal-all, lady's mantle, and motherwort.

Working on the land or in the garden carries the inherent risk of injury, from pulling muscles or ligaments, twisting a joint, or being cut or pierced by a tool or other materials we work with. For example, handling chicken wire with its sharp ends tends to draw a bit of blood even when I wear gloves. Thorny plants like black-berries, greenbrier, raspberries, barberries, and roses also often demand a blood sacrifice in return for releasing their edible gifts. The bramble thorns remind me of little sharp-toothed dragons guarding sweet treasure.

When I forget to wear gloves while pruning tomatoes, their leaves blacken my hands with a sticky residue that requires soap, hot water, and a brush to clean up. No matter how thoroughly I wash my hands, black debris remains under my fingernails for days. Other plant contact cannot easily be washed away. Brushing against poison ivy, rhubarb, squash, and strawberry leaves leads to rashes, blisters, or hives on my skin.

And then there are the insects: mosquitoes, ticks, horseflies, gnats, chiggers, hornets, yellow jackets, bees, and ants that all like to bite or sting. I accidentally ran the lawn mower over the invisible entrance to an underground yellow jacket nest. The yellow jackets chased me as I ran away flailing my arms. I ended up with several stings and days of large red swellings on my legs. I have learned to swallow quercetin capsules and sip tinctures of plantain and osha to help my body simmer down from its violent histamine reaction. Dan is not nearly as sensitive to insect bites as I am. He was stung on his face by three honeybees while mowing near our bee house. I used tweezers to pull out the stingers embedded in his cheeks and forehead, poison sacs still attached, and applied my jewelweed tincture to clean the tiny wounds and stop the itching. A few hours later, the swellings had fully receded and his face looked normal again.

For simple insect bites, we often use a spit poultice of English plantain or jewelweed leaves to relieve the itching. Spit poultice is just a fancy term for chewing a few of these medicinal leaves and mixing them with saliva, then applying the moist plant mixture to the bite.

A bull's-eye rash from a tick bite, on the other hand, requires a course of antibiotic treatment. In recent years, the dreaded deer ticks and accompanying diseases have noticeably increased, even at our higher elevation. Ticks often carry Lyme disease, Rocky Mountain spotted fever, and other diseases that have become epidemic through much of New England and the mid-Atlantic states. Daily tick checks have become mandatory for us. Muscle sprains or a twisted ankle, knee, or shoulder joint are other occasional injuries. I treat them with homemade salves made from comfrey, St. John's wort, and cannabis leaves. I regularly make another salve infused with calendula blossoms and comfrey and plantain leaves, which soothes and heals rashes and other skin maladies.

Each year, I also make a rubbing alcohol infusion from the leaves, stalks, and flowers of the jewelweed plant (*Impatiens capensis*). After the plant material has dyed the alcohol deep green, I strain it out and keep the medicinal alcohol year-round for preventing poison ivy outbreaks and treating insect bites and skin rashes.

To make an herbal salve, I cover the wilted blossoms and leaves of selected plants with grapeseed oil. After allowing this mixture to infuse for up to two months and checking frequently for any mold buildup, I strain out the plant material, gently heat the oil, and mix it with melted beeswax. Once cooled, this simple salve is soothing for a variety of skin conditions and speeds up healing.

All through spring and summer, herbs are slowly and quietly releasing their healing elements into alcohol, oil, or vinegar on my kitchen counter or drying in the dehydrator or on towels spread on the floor before being stored in glass jars. Thus, many of the herbs growing in July alleviate respiratory or allergic conditions, lift my mood during the dark times of winter, or soothe assorted aches and pains.

July Summary

Even as the sun was honored as a life-sustaining deity by many cultures in the past, the heat of the sun is becoming increasingly unbearable and life-threatening as global warming proceeds at a rapid pace. At our elevation, summer temperatures have rarely reached the low nineties, and few homes have traditionally needed air-conditioning. This is changing now. We installed an energy-efficient mini-split unit to cool our main living space on hot days. We are also beginning to see climate migration from western and southwestern states into the Appalachian mountain range and as far north as Vermont and Maine. Substantial increases in property and rental costs have ensued.

While Nature offers us ample plant medicine to heal injuries and mishaps associated with outdoor living, global warming and its repercussions will require much more profound solutions and collaboration around the world than I could offer with my home-grown remedies. Clearly beyond the scope of this book, I can only acknowledge this theme tangentially.

Journaling Prompts for Self-Reflection

1. How do you prefer to spend summer? Where? How do you deal with summer heat where you live?

2. How much of your time do you spend outdoors? What kind of activities do you enjoy? Has this changed over the years?

3. How do you and your family treat minor injuries and illnesses? Do you use plants as allies for healing? If not, why not?

4. Where does intensity show up in your life? What form does it take? When does intensity become excessive? How do you dial it down?

5. What do you do that requires physical labor, and how do you feel about performing this labor? What were the messages you received about physical labor while growing up?

AUGUST

Along the Road

Tall weeds
standing guard there
by the fence,
missed by tractors
ignored by deer
they burst into beauty
as the cars fly by.

Pink cotton candy,
bronzed velvet,
purple pompom balls,
yellow feather boas.
Who even knows
their names
as the cars fly by.

Who knows what
tea they might flavor,
what malady they might cure,
what other secrets they shelter
standing guard there
by the fence
as the cars fly by.

Excess & Abundance

August can be a month of extremes. Some years, we have sufficient rainfall and tolerable temperatures, leading to towering
garden weeds and massive amounts of squashes, beans, tomatoes,

cucumbers, and peaches. Other years, it can be very hot and dry, wilting even drought-tolerant plants and reducing crop size and amounts. Some of our neighbors' wells have dried up. It startles me how this month of copious abundance can also engender its opposite—shrinkage, wilting, even death. Most years, though, the garden, fields, and woods produce so prolifically that a good part of harvesting includes giving away or bartering the excess bounty before it spoils. I spend most August days dehydrating, freezing, and canning vegetables and fruits. Looking at the baskets full of garden produce fills me with gratitude and awe. Processing all that food, however, quickly becomes monotonous and exhausting.

When I drink my morning coffee on the porch, I notice distinct sound changes in nature: while the hummingbirds amp up their sugar water intake from the feeder, fattening up for their impending migration, and the second set of barn swallow young are preparing to leave their nest above our porch, other bird sounds have noticeably diminished. Instead, my ears are ringing with a pervasive insect soundscape, subtle during the day, much louder at night. At the end of the month, gathering for their long journey south, nighthawks with distinct white stripes on elegant pointy wings swoop through the early evening skies.

Grain Mothers & Corn Gods

In the northern hemisphere, the first day of August is the midpoint between the summer solstice and fall equinox and has traditionally been celebrated in the Celtic world as Lammas Day, Loaf Mass, or Lughnasaid (pronounced loo-nass-ah).[1] In the United Kingdom and other European countries, the grains harvested at this time included barley, wheat, oats, and rye. The loaves of bread baked from the first grains of the season were brought to church to be blessed during "Loaf Mass."[2]

Lammas, the first of three autumn harvest festivals, is dedicated to Lugh, the Celtic god of blacksmiths and other artisans. In honor of his mother, Tailtiu, Lugh initiated festivities that included fairs, games, and bonfires. It was a time for the community to gather and celebrate the fruit of their labor. Lugh, sometimes also called John Barleycorn, was multifaceted. In his role as the sun god, he was considered the living spirit of the grain. When the grain was cut down, Lugh died with it, as he transformed into the bread that fed the people through winter. He was reborn the following spring from the seed corn placed in the soil.[3]

Lammas is also dedicated to the goddess in her form as Earth Mother or Grain Mother. Corn dolls were crafted from wheat stalks to honor her and as good-luck symbols for the household. Europeans used the word *corn* as the overarching category for all grains growing in their region: wheat, oats, barley, and rye. In fact, the German word for grain is *Korn*. The corn indigenous to the Americas was called either Indian corn or maize. So the corn mothers of ancient Europe were really grain mothers or grain goddesses.[4] Ceres was the Roman goddess of the harvest. We still call grains *cereals* after her.[5]

Grain harvests have been crucially important for human sustenance since the beginnings of agriculture. Consequently, grain became associated with death and rebirth cycles since at least Sumerian times.[6] It is typically the son of the Grain Mother who dies and is resurrected in harmony with the cycles of grain cultivation. When grain is harvested, the son dies a symbolic death so that people can eat. He returns to the underworld until he reemerges when the grains sprout into new life.[7]

In many European countries where Catholicism was adopted, August 15 is observed as the Feast of the Assumption of the Virgin Mary, which commemorates Mary being received into heaven. On Assumption Day, blessings are invoked for vineyards, herbs, and grains. Traditionally, freshly gathered herbs were carried to church to be blessed and later used for medicine or bound into a sheaf and hung in the home to protect against harm. This ritual echoes ancient harvest celebrations that honored the Grain Mother.[8]

Corn, the grain of the Americas, was first cultivated over nine thousand years ago in the Mayan empire in what is now known as Mexico. According to a Mayan creation story, humans were created out of corn. They worshipped a male corn god called Hun Hunahpu, who represented birth, death, and rebirth in human life and the growing seasons. Similar to the Celtic grain god Lugh, Hun Hunahpu also dies after the corn harvest and is resurrected when corn sprouts during the next growing season.[9]

Peruvians believed all plants to be inhabited by a divine being and venerated maize, quinoa, coca, and potato mothers. Representations of these divine mothers were fashioned from ears of maize or leaves of the quinoa and coca plants, then dressed in women's clothes and worshipped, similar to the grain dolls crafted by Europeans during their grain harvest.[10]

Among indigenous tribes in North America, Corn Mother or Corn Maiden sometimes refers to a deity, sometimes to a mythological figure who gifted humans with corn (maize).[11] The story of the Corn Mother has many variations. One version tells of Corn Maiden being held hostage for six months by the Spirit of Winter and then released for six months to the Spirit of Summer, a tale very similar to the Greek Persephone/Demeter legend.[12] Even in tribes that did not have a corn mother, corn itself was viewed as a precious gift from the creator.

Rice fields throughout Asia are protected by goddesses. These earth goddesses, or rice mothers, share commonalities of having journeyed to the underworld and being associated with snakes, fertility, and abundance. In Indonesia, Dewi Sri is worshipped as the Rice Mother who protects people from hunger and controls the fate of the rice harvest by bringing monsoon rains. Dewi Sri was born from an egg formed by teardrops shed by a great serpent, the Naga god Antaboga.[13] Thailand's rice goddess, Mae Posop, is similarly honored as the goddess of fertility and abundance. In Cambodia, the rice mother is known as Po Ino Nogar, the "Great One." Not only is she revered for bringing fertility and bounty to humans, she also has dominion over the underworld and the serpent race, the Nagas, who are believed to be the progenitors of the Khmer people.[14]

I was struck by the ancient association between snakes and grain deities in so many cultures. Grain goddesses of ancient Egypt, Greece, and Rome were often depicted in the company of snakes. Koreans built altars for the snake gods who protected the granaries. Grain, as the foundational nourishment of human life, and the snake, one of the earliest goddess symbols, go hand in hand, as they symbolize the cyclical nature of existence.[15]

Snake

August around our farm is full of snake energy. One hot August day, I found a black snake trapped inside the layers of a roll of bird netting in the garden shed. Black snakes are welcome on our property, as they are nonvenomous and keep rodents in check. The trapped snake was about four feet long, and its tail was sticking out of the tangled plastic webbing. How had it gotten in there in the first place, and how long had it been trapped?

I placed the writhing bundle on the floor and held down the snake's neck with one foot while I tried to cut away the netting, which was pressing deeply into the snake's body. Soon, sweat was dripping off my face while I marveled at the strength of the muscular flesh underneath the reptile's smooth, scaly skin. I needed another pair of hands for this rescue mission, but I was alone that day, and it was entirely up to me to save this snake's life.

Finally, all the netting was cut open and I stepped back to give the snake space to escape. I was concerned about the deep ridges the plastic strings had carved into its body, though there was no blood. The snake remained still for a moment as if to make sure that it was really free. Then it slithered away, and I remembered to breathe.

Among the few poisonous snakes to look out for in our area are rattlesnakes. Rattlesnakes always surprise me when I first hear them. Sometimes, they sound like air escaping from a compressor, as the one inside our garage did. Or, like the one visiting our porch, they make a really loud cicada sound. I almost stepped on a rattlesnake while I was looking around for whatever weird insect seemed to be vibrating the air on our porch. Thankfully, I noticed the cat's cautious posture, followed her eyes, and then saw the rattlesnake between some flower-pots on the porch, coiled and in attack mode. *Whew*, I quickly stepped back.

Above all, I love finding discarded snakeskins. Often wedged between rocks, they are delicate, translucent, and almost weight-less. Sometimes, even the shape of the head and mouth are still intact. Holding such a skin feels like cradling the snake's ephem-eral spirit. One particular snakeskin nudged me to revise my life priorities. While walking through our woods, I saw some-thing dangling from a giant dead tree. Transfixed, I looked up at the thin membrane swaying like a delicate scarf from a height of about ten feet. It was the largest snakeskin I had ever come across. While I looked around cautiously for the owner of that old skin, my mind kept chanting: "Transformation, transforma-tion, time for transformation."

I remembered that in Native American mythology, snake is a symbol of transformation and healing. In Eastern lore, a coiled snake at the base of the spine represents kundalini energy, which, once activated, opens up new levels of awareness and creativity. In many cultures, snake symbolizes rebirth, initia-tion, and wisdom.

What kind of transformation was imminent in *my* life? As I contemplated and journaled over the next few days, the snake-skin released its short message to me: "Go deep. Go deep—here."

I had been spreading myself much too thin, going wide and far, and I knew intuitively what "going deep" meant: to reevalu-ate my outside activities and invest my energies into my life here, on my mountain property in Virginia. This is where I go deep, with native plants, herbal medicine, and stewarding the land and the woods.

"Go deep," the snake whispered through its cast-off skin.

Following the snake's advice, I began to shed fragments of my old skin: I dropped the majority of political activities that had been depleting my creative and emotional energies; I placed a moratorium on plane travel, which eliminated my largest carbon footprint source; and over the next several months, I purged spaces in my house by selling, giving away, or recycling unneeded items.

With my energies freed up and my house and schedule decluttered, I created a small sanctuary for endangered medicinal woodland plants, recommitted to coauthoring a book encouraging local gardeners to grow native plants, and designed workshops to help others reconnect to their outer and inner nature. I feel more anchored and grounded in my new skin, and I am listening more intently to that inner calling, all inspired by a snake's discarded garment!

August Garden & Landscape

The rich green color of grass has faded to drier, brown shades in many places. The nuanced greens of the forest trees have morphed into a dark, muddy green already showing specks of orange and red.

In the garden, heat-loving Thai Roselle hibiscus, Genovese and holy basils, and sweet peppers are thriving in the greenhouse as long as they receive daily waterings. Pattycake squash the size of small plates and zucchinis turned massive overnight need immediate harvesting. Corn ears are growing fat on the stalk but still have some empty space at the tip of the ear to fill. I look at the lush, dark-green leaves of sweet potatoes and the weeds growing up in between. Will I get around to weeding them? Or even pull up some of the healthy-looking sweet potato leaves and incorporate them into dinner? A stand of lamb's-quarter is buzzing with honeybees, their skinny legs laden with golden yellow packets of pollen sweetness. We should have a good honey harvest this year.

Cherry tomatoes dangle from branches bending them with their weight, vibrant teardrop shapes of red and yellow. Pea pods are fully pregnant and need harvesting before they turn yellow and shrivel on the vines. I pick whatever elderberries the birds have left behind on the wild bushes behind the garage.

Fields that remain unmowed turn into a colorful tapestry of blood-red cardinal flowers, magenta liatris, purple ironweed, and yellow wingstem. Moist roadside ditches draw the eye to orange jewelweed and striking blue lobelia blossoms.

FORAGED PLANT
Elderberry (*Sambucus species*)

American elderberry (*Sambucus canadensis*) is a large shrub native to North America. In late spring, it produces clouds of white creamy flowers that attract a large variety of pollinators. The flowers turn into deep purple, almost black berries in late summer.

A western version (*Sambucus caerulea*) produces blue berries with a white frosting on them. Another elderberry variety (*Sambucus racemosa*) has toxic red berries, which can induce nausea and vomiting. The black elderberry (*Sambucus nigra*), native to Europe and Asia, has now been shown to be genetically identical to the American elder.[16]

All parts of elderberry (root, leaf, stem, and seeds of the berry) contain cyanogenic glycosides. The small amounts of this toxin in the berry seeds is deactivated by cooking them.[17] I often use elderflowers for a refreshing cordial by fermenting them in sugar water and lemon juice. They can also be dipped into thin pancake batter and fried. I dry some of the flowers and reserve them for medicine. An elderflower tea can help break a fever[18] or treat a cold or flu.[19] Once cooled, the tea can be used as a gargle for sore throat.[20] Elder's high levels of antioxidants and other phytonutrients (especially anthocyanins) have been clinically proven to alleviate inflammation,[21] bring down fever,[22] and relieve allergies.[23] Elderberry syrup acts as an antiviral agent and can be used as a flu and cold preventive or at the first subtle signs of a cold. It also shortens the length of upper respiratory infections.[24]

Elderberry syrup is now widely available in the US under the name Sambucol. I make my own version of this syrup by cooking the berries in water, then mashing them and straining out the solids. I add honey to thicken the juice and to extend its shelf life. It keeps well for many months in the refrigerator, even longer in the freezer. I enjoy adding a teaspoon of elderberry juice or syrup to water and drinking it as a preventive tonic, especially when respiratory diseases make the rounds in winter. I also like to add a bit of elderberry syrup to a glass of kefir or homemade kombucha, turning it into a refreshing and delightfully pink beverage. The syrup also adds dramatic deep red color when poured over vanilla ice cream or pancakes.

Humans are not the only creatures who appreciate elder's offerings. Pollinators eagerly buzz around the flowers; deer browse its leaves and twigs; and squirrels, mice, and birds feast on its berries even before they are sufficiently ripe for human consumption.

On a cautionary note, elderberries need to be carefully differentiated from the toxic berries of devil's walking stick (*Aralia spinosa*) and pokeweed (*Phytolacca americana*).[25] Elderflowers can also be confused with the deadly white flowers of poison and water hemlocks (Wild Carrot or Apiaceae family), which grow in similar environments.[26]

Gift & Barter Economies

The abundance of fruit, vegetables, and herbs during August makes it easy, if not mandatory, to share with others. Whatever cannot be consumed or preserved for future use is passed on to neighbors, left at a gas station or the library with a sign inviting people to help themselves. This spirit of giving and sharing is very much part of gift and barter economies that bypass the use of money and credit cards.

A gift economy is a system of exchange in which goods or services are freely given with no expectation of anything in return. However, most societies that rely on gift culture do assume some kind of reciprocity in the future.

Barter, on the other hand, is a method of exchanging goods and services without the use of money as payment. For instance, a farmer may exchange a bushel of corn for a basket of apples or repair a neighbor's car in return for getting his shed painted.

In his book *Sacred Economics*, Charles Eisenstein traces the development of money from ancient gift economies to modern capitalism. He shows how our monetary system has contributed to competition and scarcity, alienation and loss of community. Money is typically generated by extracting raw materials from nature. These materials are then turned into a commodity people must pay for with money. In addition, services that in the past were provided by family or community, either as a gift or on a barter basis, have been turned into paid services by our current money system, for example, cooked foods, child and elder care, counseling, pet grooming, and general handyman services.[27]

Eisenstein observes that our sense of community weakens or entirely disappears when we rely on money economies. Commercial money transactions have become increasingly impersonal and automated. In a commodified world, there is no relationship between purchaser and store clerk/owner beyond the monetary exchange. Self-service checkouts and online purchases cut out even the limited human interaction that occurs in greeting or exchanging small talk with a cashier. Many of us feel the need to (re)create a more connected and sustainable way of life that includes personalized interactions with others and diminishes feelings of loneliness and alienation so pervasive in our present world.

Perhaps one of the most intriguing examples of a modern gift economy is the Burning Man festival, at least as it was originally envisioned. First started in the 1980s, this event has now spread to thirty-five countries around the world. Gifting is one of the ten guiding principles of Burning Man, which also include civic responsibility, personal participation, and immediacy of experience. Many of these principles attempt to counteract the alienation and disconnection we experience in a commercialized society. Everyone offers their art, performance, music, food, water, or labor with no expectation of receiving anything in return. Participants, who call themselves Burners, are encouraged to take their Burning Man experience back into the larger world to create meaningful change.[28]

Burning Man seems to be a well-intentioned endeavor based on laudable principles of gifting and leaving no trace. Ironically, bringing up to seventy thousand participants to Nevada's Black Rock desert, the installation of immense art projects only to burn them down in the end, the sheer masses of people arriving in large RVs or private jets require a large number of resources and generate considerable trash and pollution. Despite the focus on gift economy, the cost of entry tickets is high. Ironically, Burning Man has been turned into another commodity.

In our county, as in many places across the country, a gift economy has unfolded in the form of a food bank. While two individuals oversee this effort on a volunteer basis, many others contribute in the form of surplus produce or monetary funds. This food bank enterprise represents a creative weaving together of resources to help hundreds of food insecure families. Not only do people pick up food for their own household, but they often take food for neighbors who cannot afford to take time off from work or may be housebound. Some recipients process the produce they receive and then share it with others in canned or frozen form, expanding the gift economy even further and transforming themselves from receivers into givers.

What would our world, our communities, and our social experience be like if we were able to apply gift and barter methods inherent in food banks, tool libraries, community fridges, labor exchanges, and skill sharing on a much larger scale? Could we create more satisfying reciprocal interactions that honor and respect each person's needs and gifts? How can we extend the spirit of sharing the garden bounty into other spheres of society?

I have gifted or bartered whenever possible, passing on houseplants, seedlings, garden produce, showers for travelers, an old but still functional truck, broken porcelain pieces and dried gourds to artists working with these materials, flowerpots and seedling flats to a local farmer, rides for someone unable to drive, a garden tiller and other tools. In return and entirely unexpected, others have surprised me with gifts of morel mushrooms, fresh game meat, a homemade basket, plant and tree seedlings, and the use of a goat for poison ivy control. While we were in the process of building our house, a neighbor allowed us free use of his guest cabin for several months.

Giving and receiving in this manner generates gratitude and goodwill, builds neighborly relationships and a sense of community, prevents waste and purchases of big-ticket items that are rarely used, may cut down on carbon emissions, and engenders other benefits not immediately apparent.

Beyond sharing material goods and services, I wonder how we can transfer the interpersonal and community experience of gift giving and reciprocity to our relationship with nature. Nature continually gifts us with her resources, and we mostly take without returning anything. Collapsing ecosystems, galloping species extinction, global warming, and weather chaos are the results of millennia of humans relentlessly taking from nature. One-way gift giving depletes the giver. The cycle of giving and receiving must involve reciprocity.

What can we return to nature when we take her fruits, nuts, roots, minerals, fibers, trees, water, and air? Native Americans often sprinkle tobacco and express verbal thanks after partaking of nature's offerings. We can offer appreciation, gratitude, and stewardship. Of course, we should only harvest what is needed, while making sure that enough remains for animals, for the next season, even the next generation. We can plant new shrubs and trees that are native to the area and help sustain the integrity of the local ecosystem. We can study and learn from our ancestors and the remaining indigenous populations how they have tended to their ecosystems and kept them thriving for generations. This may include prescribed burns, forest gardens, irrigation schedules that consider the entire community, coppicing instead of tree cutting, and growing ancestral foods that feed the soil and the people.

On my own property, I am committed to expanding native plant species and using organic pest management techniques instead of toxic chemicals that might run off into local waterways or poison our honeybees, native pollinators, or other wildlife. I am also keeping parts of the woods and some of our fields completely wild, so nature can do as she pleases. It is so interesting to watch the progression of wild lands over time, the new wildflowers that settle in, the shrubs and trees that grow there, and the wildlife that moves in, undisturbed by human intervention.

August Summary

August's garden abundance invites generosity and sharing through giving away and bartering. A discussion of gift and barter economies nudges us to explore how sharing the garden bounty can be extended into wider community and societal spheres. We look beyond human-to-human interactions to ask how we can transform our often one-sided extractive relationship with nature into reciprocal exchanges. Snake energy holds opportunity for transformation.

Journaling Prompts for Self-Reflection

1. Have you participated in any gift or barter exchanges, formally or informally? If so, what was the experience like?

2. Are there food banks, tool libraries, community fridges, labor exchanges, skill sharing, or other types of gift and barter

systems in your community? Do you participate in any of these? If not, what prevents you from doing so?

3. What aspect of your life contains excess and abundance? What area of your life holds scarcity?

4. What symbolizes transformation for you? What initiates transformation in your life?

5. Where and how do you "go deep?" What can you relinquish in order to free up energy for what matters to you the most?

6. What are your thoughts about reciprocity with nature? Have you practiced any reciprocal actions with nature? In what form? If not, why not?

SEPTEMBER

Autumn Meadow

Grasses,
tired green, rust brown,
savannah beige,
release
the copious scent of hay.
Seed heads,
full and heavy,
drooping leisurely,
suddenly fling
their embryonic cargo far.

Grasshoppers,
prayerful, invisible,
betray their
camouflage through
mercurial lurches.

Katydids,
omnipresent, ringing in the ear,
swelling, receding:
late summer
hypnotic trance.

Harvesting, Sacred Pause

Big change is palpable this month: intensifying leaf colors, migrating birds, crisp morning temperatures, sweaters and blankets pulled from the backs of closets. Even the wind sounds different as it rustles through the thinning volume of leaves drying in the trees. From my porch each morning, I watch flocks of birds gathering in the wild cherry trees, feeding on the remaining fruit, jostling each other for space on the branches. It reminds me of my own excitement and bustling around before a big trip—gathering all the essentials, packing a suitcase, and daydreaming about what I might experience on the trip.

The fall equinox is a time of change, an opportunity to focus on what is coming to an end and what is newly emerging in our lives. Spiritual teachers use the expression "sacred pause"[1] to refer to such times that invite us to stop our whirlwind routines and to listen deeply.

A friend invited me to go kayaking on the river that runs through her property. Despite a hectic harvesting schedule, I took time to play on the water. It was a lovely, warm afternoon, and my body quickly remembered how to smoothly move the paddle and work with the currents. Gliding on the water's surface, immersed in the sounds of gurgling water and serenading insects became a peaceful, nourishing meditation.

That afternoon on the river was my mini-version of sacred pause, my opportunity to escape the daily routines and the feeling of pressure that there's never enough time to do everything I need and want to do. Dream-like, the water's currents transported me into a space untouched by time constraints or any of the concerns of the day. I felt reenergized and promised myself to set more play dates like these going forward.

Parker Palmer addresses the seeming paradox of autumn's exquisite beauty and the season giving way to winter's darkness and death: "Faced with this inevitable winter, what does nature do in autumn? She scatters the seeds that will bring new growth in the spring—and she scatters them with amazing abandon."[2]

Like Palmer, I feel an anticipation of sadness lurking just beyond the beautiful fall colors, fields of orange pumpkins, and crisp, fog-filled mornings. This melancholy is about the anticipation of winter, the dark times, my least favorite time of year.

Palmer continues, "In a culture that prefers the ease of either-or thinking to the complexities of paradox, we have a hard time holding opposites together. We want light without darkness, the glories of spring and summer without the demands of autumn and winter."[3] If I am honest, that is exactly what I want, the ease of the warmer seasons without having to drudge through cold discomfort. And, yet, according to Palmer, "If we allow the paradox of darkness and light to be, the two will conspire to bring wholeness and health to every living thing."[4]

Kat Maier, a master herbalist, describes autumn as a season of letting go, a shedding of emotions and belongings that clutter our physical and emotional spaces, and honoring the grief involved in doing so.[5]

But neither Parker's nor Maier's elegant insightful words can entirely abolish my growing sense of winter dread, though they do offer a promise and pose the question: how can we bring more peace and pleasure into our life even as the light is fading?

One of my favorite fall rituals is to deep clean my house while pondering the events of the year so far. I pull out warmer clothing and sturdier shoes, along with an additional blanket for the bed. I will miss the pleasure and freedom of having doors and windows flung wide open. As my body seeks more nourishment and warmth from heavier stews, breads, and root vegetables, I will miss the summer fare—cold soups, fruit smoothies, big salads—and the lightness and vibrancy in my body from consuming them on a daily basis. I am relieved to see the growing and harvesting season come to an end, especially the demanding physical labor of daily garden chores, even as I am wary of spending too much time indoors during the upcoming months accompanied by the dreaded seasonal depression that often catches up with me by January.

The end of September is my time to let go of accumulated physical and emotional clutter and to refine my thinking and experimentation with the theme of minimalism and enoughness in my life.

Fall Equinox & Harvest Festivals

The fall equinox in late September is the midpoint between the summer and winter solstices and the official start of autumn in the northern hemisphere. Just as during the spring equinox, night and day are once again of equal length. However, following the fall equinox, daylight is gradually diminishing by about three minutes each day as we inevitably move toward the darkest time of the year.

Among neopagans in the west, the fall equinox and its accompanying festival is now named after the Welsh god Mabon, the son of Modron, the Earth Mother goddess. While the fall equinox has been observed as an important seasonal marker since ancient times, the term *Mabon* was adopted as recently as the 1970s. Mabon celebrations often feature a cornucopia filled with the bounty of the harvest from the land.[6] The cornucopia itself is derived from the horn that symbolized the earlier mother goddess associated with a cow or goat. Fertility and abundance poured forth from her "horn of plenty."[7]

Around the globe, numerous harvest festivals are celebrated. Gratitude for the abundance of nature is one of our shared human experiences. I grew up with "New Wine" festivals held in southern Germany this time of year. The new bubbly wine was served with a type of onion pizza, a savory flatbread that complemented the sweet wine perfectly. New wine tastes a bit like sweet cider, even though it already has significant alcohol content, which makes for happy and giddy festival goers.

The Munich Oktoberfest is a well-loved festival that begins in mid-September and produces many drunken revelers by the time it ends in early October. The main attraction of Oktoberfest is beer, food, entertainment, and the spontaneous camaraderie that evolves while sitting and drinking in close proximity with thousands of other people inside huge halls. This festival began in 1810 and has only been interrupted a few times, by World War II and the COVID-19 pandemic.[8] Oktoberfest is also celebrated in American cities with substantial German-American populations, such as Cincinnati, Minneapolis, and Madison.[9]

Another popular harvest festival is the Moon or Mid-Autumn Festival held in China, Vietnam, and Taiwan. It is celebrated on the fifteenth day of the eighth month of the Chinese lunar calendar, which can fall anywhere during the month of September.[10] Favorite activities during this three-thousand-year-old festival include moon- and stargazing, lighting lanterns, and eating traditional foods, especially moon cakes.[11]

Yam festivals are joyous celebrations throughout the yam-growing region of West Africa, which includes Ghana, Nigeria, Togo, Benin, and Cote d'Ivoire. Chanting, drumming, dancing, and yam dishes are essential components of these festivals, along with competitions to determine the largest yam that will bestow upon its grower the title of yam king. Cultivation of yams began here eleven thousand years ago, and this tuber has become a life-sustaining crop. Yam festivals are also organized in cities throughout Europe, Asia, and the Americas where large numbers of West African immigrants have settled.[12]

In Israel and among Jewish communities across the globe, Succoth, or the Feast of Booths, is held this time of year. It is an eight-day harvest festival to give thanks for the fruits and grains received from the land. It also recalls the historical exodus of the Israelites from Egyptian slavery. Families build simple booths or huts, called sukkahs, re-creating the temporary dwellings of farmers during harvesting season and also symbolizing the simple shelters of the Israelites during their forty years of wandering through the desert. People often eat and sleep in these sukkahs for the duration of the holiday. Beyond thanksgiving for the harvest, Succoth is an opportunity to focus on cultural identity, spirituality, and hospitality.[13]

Indigenous practices in the Americas that honor the changes brought by the equinox include ritual cleansings. In Mexico and the Mexican diaspora, folk healers called *curanderos* or *curanderas* perform cleansing ceremonies (*limpias*) for both physical and spiritual healing during this auspicious time.[14] In the United States, many Native Americans use smudging rituals, burning sage, tobacco, juniper, sweet grass, or cedar. This scented smoke assists in cleansing the air and a person's energetic space to usher in the desired transformation for the new season.[15]

Spider

As I was driving along a country road on a September morning, I saw hundreds of spiderwebs suspended between dew-covered grasses. Backlit by the morning sun, they quivered in the slightest breeze. Tiny dew drops shimmered like rhinestone garlands. The entire scene was magical, as if the webs themselves were living, breathing entities. To the insects and moths, however, these exquisite lacy designs become death traps.

Why are so many people so afraid of spiders? There are over forty-three thousand known species of spiders, and only a few are poisonous. Among the poisonous ones, the venom of only a tiny percentage is fatal to humans.[16] Little house spiders are harmless, even beneficial, because they eat insects that hide in the crevices of our homes. I can understand the shock of coming across a giant, hairy tarantula, but a small house spider? What is it about spiders that makes us scared, even phobic? Did we learn this fear from our parents and others around us, or is there an epigenetic imprint that has accumulated in our DNA for generations? Dr. Graham Davey, a psychologist, speculated that spiders have a strong disgust and fear factor because they were associated with disease during the Middle Ages. Not only were spiders believed to be poisonous, but they were also thought to be carriers of the black plague, even though it was fleas carried by rats that brought the dreaded fatal disease. Davey found that a fear of spiders can be transmitted within families through social learning. He pointed out that the fear of spiders is not a universal phenomenon and seems to be present primarily in countries with European descendants.[17]

In the mythologies of Native America, Africa, and the African Diaspora in the Caribbean and South America, spiders are viewed quite differently. In African mythologies, the gods used strands from the spider's web to get to and from heaven.[18] The Ashanti spider trickster Anansi was the son of the earth goddess, Asaase Yaa, and the sky god, Nyame. It was Anansi who created the sun, moon, and the stars.[19] Anansi, the spider, also features prominently in Caribbean folktales where he plays a role similar to the coyote trickster in Native American lore.

The Diné (Navajo) honor Spider Woman as a supreme being who created the universe and sculpted humans out of black, red, yellow, and white-colored clays. She created the directions by spinning two gigantic threads, one running east-west, the other north-south. Spider Woman taught humans how to weave intricate tapestries and garments. Each person is seen as a strand in the vast interconnected web of life. Individual actions and thoughts affect the entire web. Through Spider Woman's gift of weaving, she enables humans to become cocreators of their destiny, to spin their own lives into a myriad of possibilities, and to create a better future.[20]

Spider Woman destroyed the world, her web, many times, and only those who remained connected with her through an invisible strand from the top of their heads were saved. This energetic thread reminds me of the Hindu concept of the seventh chakra, which resides just above the crown of the head and connects us to the divine.[21]

Ancient Peruvian cultures carved massive human, animal, and plant outlines (called geoglyphs) into the desert floor. Due to their magnitude—spread across 190 square miles—they are best visible from a plane. Among the three hundred geoglyphs, now known as Nazca lines, there is a 150-foot spider design. Most of the Nazca designs were created more than two thousand years ago, some even earlier by a culture predating the Nazca. Speculations on the purpose of these designs range from sacred paths, to elaborate rituals petitioning the gods for water, to alien landing strips.[22]

On the Native American medicine wheel, spider represents the direction of the north, wise elders and ancestors, and the season of winter. Just as autumn is the portal into winter, spider symbology hints at the opportunity opening before us as the year enters its final quarter, an invitation to turn inward, toward stillness, where we can spin the strands of the year's harvest together, gathering the many sticky threads, entangling experiences, and creative lessons into the annual web of our life.

September Garden & Landscape

A few straggling hummingbirds still visit the feeder and are finally gone by the end of the month; I heard the last call of the whippoorwill during the middle of September. Up until the final week of the month, we see flock after flock of songbirds gathering in the trees before heading south. I often think of the miracle and mystery of bird migration, the distances these birds cover, the intelligence of finding the perfect route, their bodily adjustments to help them survive a time of maximum exertion and minimal food intake.

The fields and meadows have turned into tapestries that interweave the rich autumn colors of goldenrod's sunny plumes and asters, dressed in white, pink, blue, and purple. The seed heads of summer's wildflowers, joe-pye weed, ironweed, and wingstem insert themselves as brown silhouettes into the still thriving fall flowers. Red, purple, and dark blue berries add even more color to the landscape and forest edges. Autumn olives, greenbrier, barberry, and wild rose all produce prolific amounts of berries for wildlife and foraging humans.

Here in the Virginia mountains, we often enjoy gorgeous days with temperatures in the seventies during the first half of the month. However, nighttime temperatures can easily drop into the forties, and, by the end of September, to freezing. I always feel a little anxious about my sweet potatoes, wondering whether they have had sufficient growing time. In the past, I've always dug them out of the ground before a predicted frost. But this year, I learned from a local farmer that he waits for the first frost before digging up his sweet potatoes. I will have to experiment by leaving a few in the ground to see whether they can truly survive a light frost. When I do harvest them, they are long and stout, reaching deep down into the soil, substantial and nutritious treasures for many winter meals.

Cucumbers and summer squashes have reached the end of their growing cycle, leaves wilted and infested with mildew. I am content to tear out their vines, now that we've had more than our fill of these vegetables all summer long. Each time I am in the garden this month, I leave with another "final" harvest of beans, peppers, basil, peas, beets, or carrots and another patch of barren soil to be planted later with a winter cover crop. Tomatoes keep bearing until first frost. The loofah gourds hang heavy from the bean teepee. Dill seed heads are turning brown bending the stalks with their weight. I love to prepare my own spices and spice mixtures from my garden herbs, which typically include dill leaf, dill seed, thyme, parsley, basil, nasturtium, and coriander seeds.

In the hoop house, my Roselle hibiscus, a subtropical plant, is finally producing her dark red calyxes, which I use to make a rich, spicy juice or tea. Watermelons and cantaloupes are nearly ready for harvesting. At our elevation (2,700 feet), these fruits don't receive a sufficient number of hot, sunny days to thrive in the open garden, but they do reach maturity and an acceptable level of sweetness in the greenhouse.

I frequently check on the orange pie pumpkins, butternut squashes, blue hubbards, and acorn squashes emerging from the thick cover of itchy leaves. Winter squashes remain on the ground until the last possible day before the first frost, as they increase substantially in size during their final weeks on the vine. On harvest day, I carry one heavy pumpkin after another to the water hydrant to wash and then drive them up to the house where they are scattered around the woodstove for a few weeks of curing. Curing is the process by which the outer skin thickens sufficiently to allow long-term storage in the basement through the winter months.

FORAGED PLANT

Goldenrod (*Solidago species*)

The deep yellow flames of goldenrod define the autumn landscape for us. My botanical research revealed seventeen different kinds of goldenrods in our county and over one hundred species in the Americas and Eurasia. In addition to helping bees secure their winter supply of honey, this attractive wildflower serves as a strong herbal ally for humans. Goldenrod is beneficial externally for restoring damaged skin and internally for healing our respiratory, urinary, and digestive systems. This versatile medicinal plant helps to disinfect wounds and heals burns and sores.[23] It acts as a decongestant to the upper respiratory tract in cases of flu, cold, allergies, and sinusitis.[24,25] Goldenrod's antimicrobial and anti-inflammatory compounds help heal urinary tract infections and support gall bladder and kidney health.[26] It is soothing to the digestive system and relaxes spasms and cramps.[27] Goldenrod leaves have a sweet-spicy flavor that make a tasty cup of hot tea, especially during cold and flu season. Goldenrod-infused honey helps alleviate pollen allergies. I like to cover goldenrod flowers with grapeseed oil for about two months. The resulting gold-tinged liquid, when mixed with additional plantain, yarrow, and St. John's wort–infused oils, becomes the base for a salve that heals wounds and eases body aches. The alchemy of herbal salves, tinctures, and teas transform goldenrod's multifaceted chemical compounds into valuable medicine and support for winter's health challenges.

Goldenrod has also been appreciated by fiber artists as a dye plant. The flowers impart a golden or olive-green tint to silk and wool depending on the type of mordant used in the dying process. I have enjoyed experimenting with goldenrod for dying silk scarves and homemade paper.

The various goldenrod species seem to be interchangeable for their medicinal uses. However, care must be taken when foraging goldenrod, as there are a number of poisonous plants in the *Senecio* and *Packera* families that resemble it, such as groundsel and ragwort.[28,29]

What Is Enough?

Nature's abundance and our sharing of harvest surplus to prevent waste raise the questions: *What is enough?* and *Who doesn't have enough?* How do we enable access to sufficient food and other necessities to all people around the country and the world? Especially now, as we must minimize fossil fuel use and rethink national and global priorities to reign in global warming. Especially now, as the excesses of resource extraction and consumption in the industrialized nations have led the entire planet to the brink of mass extinction of flora and fauna, and runaway global warming fuels monster storms and ever more habitat destruction.

When Dan and I first moved to our land in the Virginia Highlands, we naively expected a more simple existence than our earlier suburban Washington, DC, life allowed.

Our newly acquired property consisted of fifty-eight acres of fields and woods. We had a road built, a well drilled, underground electric cables and telephone lines installed. Once we moved into our house, which is heated by a woodstove, there was firewood to be cut and stored for winter. Chainsaw and tractor to the rescue, along with a wood splitter.

When Dan first ordered the tractor with its various attachments, I teased him about his "big toy" acquisitions and wondered out loud whether they were necessary. Today, we could not imagine life on our homestead without them. Still, they leave me conflicted: these machines require fossil fuels to operate, which is exactly what we all need to reduce or eliminate. While we purchased a battery-powered weed whacker and an electric lawnmower, there are no easy alternatives to the larger gas-guzzling machines. The romantic fantasy of rural life wears off quickly when you are faced with the many daily tasks that keep a homestead functioning, even with modern machinery and other labor-saving devices. And as we both move into our elder years, our decreasing energy levels and more limited physical abilities require even more accommodations. Is our rural lifestyle sustainable?

I calculated that our annual carbon footprint is about 50 percent below the average American household at our income level. We generate about 75 percent of our annual electricity needs from solar panels on the ground and heat our water with rooftop solar panels. Still, we use a lot of gasoline for mowing and transportation. We live an hour's drive from the nearest town, where I stock up on quality groceries, go to the YMCA and a great public library, and recycle plastics. How can I bring down my fossil fuel use living in a county with no public transportation? We recently replaced our thirteen-year-old Subaru that blew its head gasket with a hybrid vehicle that gets much better mileage.

Still, I feel conflicted because I know how close we are to irreversible climate tipping points, just a few decimal points on the thermometer. Some of these tipping points will cause earth changes for centuries, perhaps even millennia, to come. The 2021 report of the Intergovernmental Panel on Climate Change (IPCC) confirms that we are currently consuming 1.7 times the resources that the earth can provide in the longterm, an entirely unsustainable state of affairs.[30]

David Korten, author and member of the Club of Rome, an organization addressing global warming and limits to growth, wrote, "The current economic system is far better suited to growing the financial assets of billionaires than to securing for all access to food, water, healthcare, vaccines, and other necessities. Living far beyond the means of a finite living Earth, we face a monumental civilizational challenge."[31] Korten specifies three interconnected steps to secure a viable future: acknowledge the limits of earth's capacities, commit to an equitable sharing of resources, and restore a healthy earth for current and future generations. He also reminds us that by embracing our ancestors' knowledge of the "inherent interdependence of life," now confirmed by many scientific disciplines, we must make the necessary changes within this decade, and no later than the early 2030s.[32]

Climate change is a merciless taskmaster that requires an urgent assessment of how we conduct our lives and necessitates immediate corrective and remedial action on an individual, corporate, and governmental level. How do we each minimize being a burden to the earth through our sheer existence? How much are we willing to change, to downscale, to reorient our life's priorities? And how can we do this together to catapult individual actions into the collective action required for planetary changes? What will motivate billionaires and multinational corporations responsible for large-scale pollution and resource use to want to create a cleaner, more sustainable world that meets the needs of everyone?

Perhaps the most comprehensive resource I have come across in pursuit of answers is Paul Hawken's book *Regeneration: Ending the Climate Crisis in One Generation*.[33] In this monumental work, he addresses the challenges faced by the major bioregions on earth and describes solution-focused interventions that have stopped and even reversed environmental destruction and pollution. Jam-packed with both sobering facts and promising, research-based solutions, Hawken's book left me feeling empowered and encouraged that my individual actions to reduce my carbon (and methane) footprint are indeed meaningful and essential. Hawken also shows how areas not usually viewed within the context of climate change are in fact connected to it. These include human rights, gender and economic justice, abolishing poverty, and reparations to formerly colonized people. There is no artificial dichotomy between environmental work and efforts to improve people's lives. Hawken and his team of activists, researchers, and writers have created an extensive website (https://regeneration.org/) where you can read more, use a carbon calculator to assess your own lifestyle, create an action list uniquely suited to your life circumstances, and feel inspired by a worldwide network of people committed to reversing the climate crisis facing us all.

September Summary

As harvest festivals all over the world celebrate the abundant blessings from the land, nature gives us many farewell presents before she prepares to rest in the cold months ahead: not only food that can be stored but also medicinal plants to prepare for winter's challenges. The fall equinox provides an opportunity for sacred pause, to lean into the teachings held by the dark and cold.

Spider lore holds a profound metaphor for creation and the interweaving of the facets of our lives into a larger tapestry, our planet being the extraordinary mélange of elements that form the foundation of our existence. This leads us into the exploration of what is enough and where we can limit our consumption and pivot toward minimizing our impact on the earth's ecosystems.

Journaling Prompts for Self-Reflection

1. How are you personally impacted by climate change?

2. If you were told that the planet will fail to sustain life as we know it in five years, what would you do differently today?

3. What's preventing you from taking that planet-saving action right now?

4. What are your thoughts about what is enough in your own life? What actions have you taken to minimize your own consumption and/or share what you have with others?

5. Are you grieving anything or holding grudges or resentments that need releasing before winter?

6. What would you like to focus on as the year is winding down?

OCTOBER

Essence

Chisel me like the rock,
strip away
the powder puffs of ego,
loosen
the aching tendons of control,
pry off
the veneer of education,
blow away
the dressy layers of civilization.

Chisel me into
breathing, sculpted essence,
until I am
naked and windswept,
until I remember
who I was and
who I am to be now.

Ancestral Connections, Releasing

In early October, brilliant leaf colors fill me with marvel and gratitude. Then, suddenly, we awaken one morning to a stiff, frosted landscape. Within just a few hours following the first night of a hard frost, walnut and locust trees drop their still substantial volume of leaves and expose their naked branches to the chilly air. The fallen leaves form a perfect circle around the trunks, like a silky robe slipped off carelessly.

For me, this month is marked by the anniversary of my mother's passing, a stark reminder of the season coming to a close. She had been suffering from bone cancer. I was surprised how the news of her death unsettled me. I felt unbalanced physically, as memories of my mother rolled through my mind in waves. It dawned on me later that I was adjusting to a new reality, the reality of now being one of the elders in my family, with very few people remaining from my parents' generation. Even though I had been independent from the age of seventeen, and there was an entire decade when I was not in communication with my mother, we had reconnected in recent years, and I was aware of her deterioration. At the time of her death, it had been five years since I had seen her last. Because of the COVID pandemic, I chose not to fly to Germany for a final visit.

My mother's passing makes me even more attuned to the original meaning of Halloween: remembering the dead and honoring them as our ancestors. I feel humbled, aware of edging closer to the ancestral line myself. With my mother gone from this life, I have no one ahead of me as a buffer between this life and the afterlife. Her death has been the primary rite of passage into my own elderhood.

A dozen people in my life died the same year my mother passed: my ex-husband, aunts and uncles, friends and acquaintances. Members of my parents' generation were the knowledge keepers, though many of them chose to be secret keepers, reluctant to talk about the past. My oldest aunt is the only person left who is able and willing to answer questions about my family's past. She has graciously filled in major gaps in my knowledge of my grandparents' lives and the trickling down of family dynamics. I am writing about my own memories of poignant family events for my grandchildren, so they do not have to play detective to access our family history.

In October, I usually take a solo vacation from my life on the homestead. I love to spend time by the ocean for much-needed rest, perspective, and rejuvenation. In my new environment, I ponder what wants to be shed this coming winter, what needs to die down to the ground and become fertilizer for new growth. What do I need to release to move forward? Plants and animals can teach us about death as an inherent part of the life cycle even as the landscape, the wind, and the gray clouds are talking to us in whispers. My inner landscape of loss and transition very much resembles the outer landscape that has now lost the vibrancy of summer and is moving rapidly toward the inertia of winter.

Samhain, Halloween & Day of the Dead

Samhain (pronounced sow-en), at the tail end of October, is one of the great festivals of the Celtic Wheel of the Year. It celebrates the end of the harvest season with the final gathering of nuts and fruit. Samhain also marks the beginning descent of the year into darkness. The Celtic Sun King dies and Modron, the earth goddess, now in her form as the Crone (or Cailleach), mourns his passing until he rises again at Yule time.[1]

Symbols of Samhain include the apple, representing life and immortality; the cauldron, as the container for life and death; a besom broom for ritually sweeping out the old energies so that new energies can enter the cleared space; and the acorn, symbolizing wisdom, strength, and longevity inherited from the mother tree, the revered oak.[2]

Samhain marks the beginning of the Celtic new year and is considered an auspicious time when the veil between our visible, physical world and the invisible world of the dead, the realm of the ancestors, opens for those who seek to communicate with the spirit world.

Christine Valters Paintner, a Christian mystic, describes Samhain as a threshold time that invites us to "listen for the voices we may not hear during other times of year. These may be the sounds of our own inner wisdom or the voices of those who came before us. . . . We tend to neglect our ancestral heritage in our culture, but in other cultures remembering the ancestors is an intuitive and essential way of beginning anything new. We don't recognize the tremendous wisdom we can draw upon from those who have traveled the journey before us and whose DNA we carry in every fiber of our bodies. We carry not just their wounds but also their resilience and courage as well."[3]

In the United States, children and adults wear costumes for Halloween, which is observed on October 31. For a day, they transform into witches, demons, ghosts and goblins—or superheroes. Children go door-to-door in their neighborhoods and collect sweets. Communities create haunted houses with cauldrons, skeletons, bloody scenes, graveyards, and scary zombie characters for spooky entertainment. Many people no longer know the ancient origins of Halloween when dressing up in ghost costumes and masks which originally served to confuse and evade undesirable elements visiting from the spirit world.

While it resembles Halloween, Mexico's celebration of *Día de los Muertos*, or Day of the Dead, is not its equivalent. Instead, it is a two-day celebration that honors deceased family members and is filled with socializing, dancing, and parades. *Día de los Muertos* begins on the first day of November, overlapping with the Catholic All Saints' Day. However, the festival predates Catholic colonial influence by several thousand years and has its origins in ancient Aztec celebrations that venerated Mictēcacihuātl, queen of the underworld. The Aztecs believed that the deceased temporarily return to earth during this time. In modern-day Mexico, joyful celebrations include people dressing up as skeletons with artfully painted skull faces. Altars dedicated to dead family members overflow with special foods and beverages, family photos, and marigold flowers.[4]

Squirrel

One October day, after completing a forest bathing program with a group of people, I spent some time alone under the trees. Two squirrels scampered among the leaves on the ground. The first one rocketed up the tree closest to me and disappeared into the treetops. The second squirrel, however, noticed me standing there. It interrupted its climb, clung to the tree bark, and continued to look at me, slowly wagging its head from side to side. We locked eyes for quite awhile before the little creature followed the first squirrel into the tree crown. A gentle breeze swept through and leaves twirled down around me, showering me in the process. It felt like an initiation of sorts, a gentle caressing from the trees and the squirrels, almost as if they were thanking me for doing my work among them.

Among the sixty-five squirrel species recorded in the United States, there are tree squirrels, flying squirrels, and ground squirrels, which include chipmunks and prairie dogs. The Virginia Department of Wildlife Resources lists the following five species of the tree and flying kind in our state: gray squirrel, red squirrel, fox squirrel, northern flying squirrel, and southern flying squirrel.

The most common squirrel throughout North America and Virginia is the gray squirrel, which is often found in cities where they establish habitat in hardwood trees planted along streets or within parks. In the wild, gray squirrels prefer mixed hardwood and conifer forests. They will remain inside their nests for days during rainy or cold weather.[5]

Red squirrels, about the size of chipmunks, are easily recognizable by their reddish gray back and white belly. In Virginia, they prefer the higher elevations of the western mountain range, where they make themselves at home in pine and spruce forests. They are particularly vociferous, chattering incessantly, especially when disturbed.[6]

Fox squirrels are larger than gray squirrels and relatively common in most counties west of the Blue Ridge Mountains in Virginia, as well as many other parts of North America, including southern Canada and northern Mexico. This species makes dens in hollow tree trunks and limbs. They favor open woodlots and forest borders and forage on the ground during daytime.[7]

The Virginia northern flying squirrel, on the other hand, depends on a specific habitat that has been shrinking over the decades: red spruce forests at elevations above 3,000 feet. Remnants of these red spruce forests remain primarily in West Virginia and only two mountainous counties in Virginia, including our own Highland County. This nocturnal animal is an extremely hardy species that is active even in very cold and harsh weather.[8] This particular squirrel was on the list of rare animals threatened by the proposed construction of an industrial wind turbine farm on a remote mountain ridge in our county. The construction would have occurred in an area that not only spawns the headwaters of three watersheds but also supports plants and animals not found elsewhere in the region, including birds, bats, snowshoe hare, salamanders,[9] and our Virginia northern flying squirrel. After years of active opposition by a coalition of environmentalists, scientists, and lawyers, the wind turbine project was abandoned. This was my introduction into the complexities of environmental politics.

The southern flying squirrel, not quite as demanding in its habitat needs as its northern flying cousin, is at home in mixed hardwood forests at any altitude throughout Virginia and eastern North America. It is nocturnal and is the most carnivorous of the squirrels mentioned. Aside from the usual squirrel diet consisting of flowers, fruit, berries, fungi, lichen, nuts, and tree bark, it also adds insects and their larva, baby birds, and small snakes to this smorgasbord.[10] Flying squirrels do not actually fly, they glide, or more specifically, they volplane. Stretchy folds of skin membranes that extend on both sides of the body from wrist to ankle act like sails when the squirrel launches itself from its powerful hind legs. "Flights" can cover distances of up to one hundred yards.[11]

Squirrels are delightful and entertaining to watch, especially when they engage in accomplished acrobatics to extract food from bird feeders. They can become quite daring in approaching people for food in city parks or other human-dominated spaces.

Their rapid chattering sometimes resembles scolding. Squirrels can also become a nuisance and cause significant damage by eating garden crops, chewing on the bark of trees and shrubs, burrowing into containers, and entering attics or house walls.[12] I have noticed many fewer squirrels on our property than in the urban and suburban environments where I've lived in the past. Perhaps the abundant presence of predators including foxes, owls, and hawks keeps their population in check and prevents them from becoming pests.

I chose this member of the rodent family as my October animal because squirrels are well-known for their expertise in storing food for winter. They collect acorns and other nuts in late fall and store them in hundreds of locations. Relying on their excellent memory, they retrieve them through the winter months. A squirrel collects between three thousand and ten thousand nuts each year. Amazingly, they are masters at differentiating which nuts will last through winter storage and which ones are better eaten in the moment. For example, an acorn from a white oak tree tends to sprout quickly after it is buried and then becomes unsuitable for food. An acorn from a red oak, on the other hand, contains higher levels of tannins and does not sprout as quickly, so it can safely be buried and eaten later in winter.[13] This reminds me of learning the hard way that yellow onions are much better winter keepers than red onions, which tend to spoil quickly in storage.

Squirrels are protective of their stored food supplies and are capable of deceiving potential competitors. When they notice another animal that may be interested in eating their buried food, squirrels pretend to deposit nuts into a particular place but then secretly take the food to another location to fool the observer.[14]

Food storage and other winter preparations are often vitally important to survival for animals and humans alike. Metaphysically, squirrel behavior can teach us not only to gather food and other essentials to prepare for times of scarcity, but also to harness our energies, our thoughts, emotions, and creative ideas and to hold them securely until they are ready to be expressed and shared with others.[15] The habit of accumulating too much and the inability to let go of things as needed is a squirrel habit gone rogue. The preponderance of storage units and the number of possessions cluttering our homes are indicators of our unhealthy relationship with things. No wonder we love to watch reality shows where decluttering experts return order and serenity to other people's living quarters. Do we fear not having enough and therefore hold on to too much? Do we lose track of what we bring into our space and then feel overwhelmed as clutter takes up more and more of our homes? Finding the happy medium between having too little or too much time, money, energy, or material things can be a formidable challenge for us modern humans.

October Garden & Landscape

During the first half of the month, our mountain ridges are aflame with brilliant reds, saffron, copper, and bronze. I am enraptured by this exquisite beauty all around me and let it soak into my cells, knowing how fleeting it is. Later in the month, the riotous colors fade into subdued red, ochre, and brown. Eventually, the trees are entirely bare after releasing their leafy garments to the compost layer of the soil.

After the first few frosty nights, most of the remaining vegetable plants in the garden have turned into slime that oozes back into the ground. Swiss chard and kale leaves, however, still wave healthy leaves in the breeze. To my surprise, the artichokes maintain their silvery green leaves.

For me, the end of gardening season is a bittersweet relief. Now it is time to process whatever food I was able to rescue from frost by turning apples into applesauce, canning pears in light syrup, making pesto and sauerkraut, and freezing peas and carrots for future meals.

The flower garden isn't entirely dead: monkshood is in full bloom. I love her deep blue color, so rare in nature. Monkshood's blousy blossoms resemble medieval hoods. When I watch honeybees enter the flowers, I wonder whether the plant's deadly poison could find its way into our honey. Responding to my panicked email, our beekeeper assuages my fear by sending me several scientific articles stating that this is an unlikely possibility. Another poisonous plant, pokeweed, still dangles its shiny black berries from thick red stalks. Calendula, French hollyhock, and native asters continue blooming undeterred by the cold nights.

We gather Chinese hybrid chestnuts that have dropped to the ground, still embedded in their spiky shells. They prick my hands even through leather gloves. We store them in two massive buckets in the shed. I hope that their thorny exterior will dry up and shrink back in a few weeks, making it easier to remove the tasty nuts.

I can't help but think that Nature's flamboyant beauty this month serves as an extravagant consolation prize for what is to come next: the dormancy and death of winter.

FORAGED PLANT

Hawthorn (*Crataegus species*)

Hawthorn is a shrub or small tree in the large rose family that also includes apple, cherry, peach, raspberry, and strawberry. More than a thousand species of hawthorn proliferate in the temperate northern parts of the world. Trees grow ten to fifty feet tall and often feature long, sharp thorns on their branches. Hawthorns like to grow along forest edges and hedgerows where they provide shelter and food for insects, birds, amphibians, and small mammals. They are also popular as ornamental shrubs, for their early spring blossoms and strikingly colorful fruits in fall.[16,17]

Because they easily interbreed, exact species can be difficult to identify. Luckily, hawthorn species are interchangeable for edible and medicinal purposes. All parts of the hawthorn tree are beneficial throughout the growing season: blossoms in spring, leaves in spring and summer, and berries/pomes in late fall. The "berries" are technically called *pomes* and resemble miniature apples.[18]

Hawthorn is particularly prominent in European folklore. The roots of these trees are said to hide the entrance to the fairy world. It is considered bad luck to chop down a hawthorn tree, as doing so will arouse the wrath of the fairy folk. The flowering branches were used to decorate homes and protect them against evil spirits. Hawthorn trunks were selected as maypoles for Beltane dances, and the white flower petals were woven into wreaths crowning the girls and women who participated in these springtime celebrations.[19]

I love seeing the creamy white petals infused with pink bloom in spring. The berries reach peak potency in October, when they turn a deep red. I rarely find them in prime condition; mostly, they are marked by insect damage when I come across them. When I do find a tree bearing unblemished fruit, I happily harvest as much as I can.

With a sweet-tart taste profile, hawthorn berries, flowers, and leaves can be prepared in a variety of ways, including candy, soup, tea, juice, wine, jam, butter, chutney, and relish.[20] Hawthorn-infused honey or vinegar acquires a pleasing rose-pink color.[21] I once came across a forager who ground the dried berries into a striking red flour.

Hawthorn has a long history of medicinal use by Native Americans and in both Western and Chinese herbal medicine. Native Americans preferred hawthorn for gastrointestinal issues, such as diarrhea, dysentery, and bloating and for controlling heavy menstrual bleeding. They also used the long thorns to lance boils and for other medicinal applications.[22]

Western medicine tends to focus on hawthorn's heart-healing qualities. Traditional Chinese medicine relies on hawthorn primarily as a remedy for spleen, stomach, and liver issues.[23] James Duke refers to several European studies that support hawthorn's mediating impact on several heart conditions. It can moderate mild angina, a heart disease that often results in chest pain upon exertion. Angina is caused by plaque accumulation in the coronary arteries.[24] Hawthorn widens the coronary arteries, thereby improving blood and oxygen flow to the heart.[25] It has also been shown effective in treating irregular heartbeat (cardiac arrhythmia). As a heart tonic and strengthener, hawthorn can help prevent heart attacks.[26] Because of its ability to improve circulation, hawthorn also helps mitigate intermittent claudication, a narrowing of the arteries of the legs that causes leg pain and impaired mobility, especially in older people.[27]

Contrary to an earlier assumption that the berries contain the most medicinal value, we now know that the flowers and leaves of hawthorn contain higher levels of flavonoids than the fruits. It is these flavonoids that assist in improving cardiac performance, reducing blood pressure, and lowering blood cholesterol levels.[28]

All parts of hawthorn can be consumed safely by anyone who wants to support their heart health except for individuals who take digitalis as medicine for congestive heart failure and cardiac weakness because hawthorn compounds the effects of digitalis.[29] If you have a serious medical condition, especially involving the heart, you should always consult a qualified medical practitioner.

Hawthorn has a calming effect on the nervous system for adults and helps children with attention deficit disorder stay more focused. It also reduces stress-induced anxiety and irritability[30] and calms down people with type A personality who tend to be aggressive and driven.[31] As a flower essence, hawthorn heals and soothes the emotional heart, especially when we are dealing with grief and loss.[32,33] Thus, hawthorn's essence leads us into the next section: facing loss and death in nature.

Death & Dying in Nature

Living close to nature isn't only filled with feel-good experiences. Pain and death are equally part of the deal. Not only have we had our share of injuries ourselves, but we have also witnessed injury and death in the animals around us. While we are more attuned to death at this time of year, reminders that death is a part of life linger all year round.

On a walk around our property, we found the sun-bleached leg bone of a deer suspended from a fence. The hoof had become entangled in the upper part of the fence. The rest of the skeleton was gone. I can't imagine the terror and pain of this poor creature, helplessly dangling from the fence before it died. We also found a bony bear claw, knuckle joints still attached, somewhere in a field. No trace of the rest of the animal anywhere.

Our semi-feral cats occasionally leave dead birds on the porch, presumably as a "gift." Once it was a male indigo bunting, left lifeless right in front of the entrance door. I love these turquoise-colored birds, and only see a few of them each year. My heart broke a little, and I yelled at the cats for the rest of the day. Sometimes, birds fly into our windows and drop on the ground, dazed and immobile. When I hear the telltale thump, I run outside to gather up the unfortunate bird before the cats snatch it up. We have rescued and revived quite a few hummingbirds and songbirds this way.

In the US alone, it is estimated that cats kill an estimated 1.3 to 4.0 billion songbirds each year, making them the number one threat to birds.[34] While our semi-feral cats earn their keep by dispatching field mice, chipmunks, and baby rabbits, they also kill a heartbreaking share of birds. Birds have many additional predators, especially snakes. I came across a black snake in the process of swallowing a young robin in its nest. The parents kept dive-bombing the snake, anguish and horror in their voices. I have never seen so much emotion in birds. The strange quiet after a bird nest is robbed of its young lingers for days.

Our two dogs roam freely inside a large, fenced territory in front of the main house that protects our beehives from bears and orchard trees from deer and raccoons. As affectionate as these dogs are with humans, they are killing machines to other animals. One of our cats made the mistake of wandering into their territory and was mauled so badly that she succumbed to her internal injuries. Occasionally, we find dead opossums, skunks, small snakes, and toads that were likely killed by our dogs. We gave up keeping chickens because our dogs massacred most of them for sport.

In addition to the role of predation and other natural causes of death in nature, I would be amiss if I did not also acknowledge our own role in nature's demise, our human impact on the death of other species, and the depletion of the natural resources we ourselves rely on to survive as a species.

I am wondering whether the losses we witness in nature—animals to the food chain, a tree in a windstorm, rare native plants to roadside mowing, or garden plants to voracious rabbits—help us prepare for what we often experience as more deeply significant losses in our lives. The loss of loved ones, the loss of a business or a career, the loss of property through natural disaster or theft, the loss of our good health impacting our daily functioning and level of independence—all of these are common human experiences that often precede our ultimate loss, our own death.

I recently spoke to an elder who had helped her brother transition in his home. She cleaned his room, brought in flowers and a bowl of fresh water, and sat with him for days until the time of his last breath. She described her witnessing and holding space for her brother's sacred passage with such tenderness that we both had tears in our eyes.

I can only hope to approach the death of a loved one, and my own inevitable demise, with similar reverence. For practice, I can learn to accept and embrace this seasonal dying, this passage into winter, with more equanimity.

October Summary

As the growing cycle is coming to a close, October is full of reminders that life is finite. The dying down of plants and the quieting of animal life naturally invites us to reflect on loss and acknowledge our need to grieve. Many indigenous cultures ritually honor and celebrate the passing of loved ones, the ancestors, as an essential part of life. Both animal and plant energies can assist us in this process. Squirrel energy carries great symbolism for preparing for loss and hard times and balancing the need to hold on versus letting go. Hawthorn's flower essence helps us move through grief and loss more gently and provides a parting gift of its fruit to take into the starkness of winter with us. October is all about gathering up, while at the same time learning to let go.

Journaling Prompts for Self-Reflection

1. What areas of your life want to be shed this coming winter, what needs to become fertilizer for new growth? What do you need to release to move forward?

2. What can plants and animals teach us about death as an inherent part of the life cycle?

3. What are grieving and mourning rituals in your family and in your community that you find helpful in processing loss?

4. Do you experience eco-grief (sadness over the loss of environmental damage and climate change)? How do you address this form of grief?

NOVEMBER

Descent

After days of heavy rain,
gray clouds lift reluctantly.
The land remains sodden, sighing heavily.
Moisture rises like smoke signals from the hollows.
I wait for clear vision.

Darkening of Days, Winter's Doorstep

November in the Virginia Highlands marks the beginning of a long, five-month stretch of winter. Goodbye to flowers, green trees, and grasses. Goodbye to long hours of outdoor time and the freedom of light clothing. I feel the loss of color, light, and warmth acutely, the main reason winter is my least favorite season.

Even on cold November days, I like to sit on our porch in the mornings. Wrapped in a blanket, I breathe in the spicy aroma of damp leaves decaying on the ground, the sweet scent of wood-stove smoke rising from the chimney, and the rustic smell of freshly cut wood stacked four feet high against the porch railing. Rain saturates what colors remain in the landscape: deep, coppery red on oaks, who hold onto their leaves longer than most other trees, cinnamon brown of sedge grasses, and the sandy plumes of ornamental grasses in the garden.

The frequent rains and occasional snowfall this month gently soak the dry earth and replenish the water table underground. During the first heavy hoar frost, I am intrigued by the shapes of snowflakes on my car windshield and examine the geometry of each one searching for a deeply ingrained blueprint, an underlying sacred pattern. A temperature drop to 18 degrees Fahrenheit leaves no doubt that winter is marching up the driveway, setting up camp outside our front door. Winter is here; deal with it!

Daylight savings time ends in early November. My internal biorhythm takes a long time to adjust to darkness descending an hour earlier. I am also reminded of what looms ahead for me: a mild to moderate case of seasonal affective disorder, also known as winter depression.

Seasonal affective disorder (SAD) is caused by our internal biological clock, our circadian rhythm being out of step with sunlight. This circadian rhythm is regulated by a tiny mechanism in the brain, the suprachiasmatic nucleus (SCN).

In the past, people received sufficient light exposure because they worked and played outside, where sunlight is one thousand times more intense than indoor lighting. This natural light intensity signaled the SCN to be active, thereby regulating our mood and supporting biological functions. Now the average American spends 93 percent of their life indoors or in vehicles, so it shouldn't be a surprise that most of us have developed light deficiencies, a condition called *malillumination*. One of the most well-known effects of insufficient ultraviolet light from the sun is vitamin D deficiency. Another is the circadian rhythm disruption that results from too little blue light in the morning and too much artificial light at night. Malillumination affects our brain, hormones, organs, immune system, mood, and energy levels and is linked to heart disease, cancer, and neurodegenerative disease. Our circadian rhythm requires not only exposure to the right kind of lighting but also exposure at the right time in any given twenty-four-hour cycle.[1]

I find it remarkable that sunlight therapy was used in India three thousand years ago. And long before that, our sun-worshipping ancestors sensed the life-giving importance of sunlight.[2]

I stock up on my supply of vitamin D3 and St. John's wort tablets and pull out my light therapy lamp for gray mornings. The lamp mimics the sun with 10,000 lux of full-spectrum light. These preventive remedies usually keep my SAD symptoms of lethargy, moodiness, and irritability at tolerable levels. And now that I know our woodstove provides me with a generous amount of red and near-infrared light, I appreciate its warmth even more. I curl up warm and cozy nearby, read and daydream into deep inner space while the Old Crone gets ready to govern the winter world outside.

The Dark Goddess: The Cailleach, Baba Yaga, Oya

In ancient European mythology, winter was ruled by a powerful old woman, the dark goddess, the Crone. She was known as the Cailleach (pronounced kahl-yach) in the British Isles, Baba Yaga in Eastern Europe, and Frau Holle in the Germanic areas.

Cailleach is a pre-Christian Celtic goddess of Ireland, Wales, and Scotland. It is believed that she originated in the Mediterranean. A temple dedicated to a giant goddess was built on the island of Malta between 3600 and 3000 BCE. As the Celts migrated from southern Europe to the British islands, this giantess turned into the Cailleach. She arrived carrying gigantic rocks that she flung across the land, creating the mountains, lakes, and rivers. The Cailleach as the old winter queen is unique to the British Isles, but she shares similar attributes with the Germanic goddess Frau Holle, or Frau Holda.[3] Much of Frau Holle's rule as an ancient goddess is lost. Her status has been diminished to the fairy tale figure of a kindly old woman who shakes out her pillowcases, thereby showering the land with snow.

Perhaps an even more ancient dark goddess is Oya, who is venerated in West Africa, the Caribbean, and Brazil. Oya is the caring and benevolent protectress of women. She also wields a sword, commands big storms, and turns into a vengeful warrior when punishing injustice. As the guardian of life and death, she is invoked during funerals and spirit communications.[4]

Barbara Walker construes the Crone as an essential component of the Triple Goddess consisting of the Maiden (as Creator), the Mother (as Preserver), and the Crone (as Destroyer). This primordial divine trinity was revered by cultures around the world, including India, the Middle East, and Mediterranean and Celtic areas.[5] Crone meant *holy one* and is related to the word *crown*, representing the highly respected position of the ancient matriarch who developed the moral codes and laws for her community.[6]

Early Christians continued to revere the Crone goddess in the form of Sophia (Wisdom), the Pneuma, or Holy Spirit, or the grandmother of God. Later in Christianity, her female essence was transformed into the masculine Holy Ghost.[7] The Christian church officially allowed the veneration of the Virgin Mary/Mother of God around the fifth century, ceding to pressures from a population still attached to the old goddess religions. The Virgin Mary and Mother of God can be seen as a continuation of the maiden and mother aspects of the Triple Goddess.[8]

The crone aspect of the goddess, however, was vilified. The once respectful term *hag* became a derogatory synonym for the fearsome witch. The demonization of the wise old woman reflected patriarchal societies' increasing suppression of women, culminating in the five-hundred-year-long stake-burning fever between the twelfth and nineteenth centuries.[9]

The Old Crone or Dark Goddess survived as an archetype in disguised form. The Baba Yaga, for example, is well known in Slavic and Baltic countries. A powerful and terrifying force of nature, she is the guardian of life and death and capable of bringing the dead back to life. In that capacity, she very much resembles the Yoruba goddess Oya. Clarissa Pinkola Estés interprets the power of the Dark Goddess and her significance for us modern women in her groundbreaking book, *Women Who Run With the Wolves*: "To face the wild power in ourselves is to gain access to the myriad faces of the subterrene feminine . . .the ogress, the witch, the wild nature, and whatever other *criaturas* and aspects the culture finds awful in the psyches of women are the very blessed things which women need most to retrieve and bring to the surface."[10]

According to Estés, women's ancient wild powers include our deep intuition, our creative fire, our ability to make forceful decisions, to bring forth life, and to end it. By learning to differentiate between what is essential and what is not, we determine what needs to be abolished, or left to die. We especially must be willing to sacrifice (let die) our culturally acquired tendency to deny our authentic self, our primordial female essence. The Cailleach and the Baba Yaga stories can give us the courage to embrace the ancient crone archetype that has (almost) been burnt out of our female psyche.[11]

Crow/Raven

Crows and ravens are members of the Corvidae family, which also includes jays and magpies. While similar in appearance, crows and ravens do differ in their size, the shape of beak and tail feathers, and social habits. The smaller crow is a gregarious, social animal, while the larger raven tends to be solitary. Even their sounds are somewhat different, at least to the trained birder's ear: crow sounds resemble a *caw*, while ravens produce a more croaking *cr-r-ruck* or a metallic *tok*.[12]

Crows and ravens have a wide range of sounds. They can imitate other bird species and can learn to speak human words. Highly observant, they can recognize individual humans. They skillfully use tools such as stones or twigs. Their intelligence and resourcefulness enable them to adapt to a variety of environments and food sources. Crows designate "watch birds" who not only warn their own but also other birds and animals of predators.[13] I often see them gang up on an eagle or a hawk, screeching loudly and dive-bombing the intruder until it leaves their territory.

The most striking quality of both crows and ravens is their deep black color, sometimes tinged iridescent purple when the light hits them just right. It is their intense black coloring that has given rise to much mystique and fear. During my childhood in southern Germany, my mother sometimes threatened me and my brothers with a stern warning: "If you don't behave, the *Nachtkrabb* will come and get you." *Nachtkrabb* was the dialect word for raven, our equivalent of the bogeyman who came at night to punish disobedient children. My early indoctrination was augmented by fairy tales that associated crows and ravens with evil witches. No wonder I disliked these corvids until I learned more about them.

Crows and ravens appear in the mythologies of many different cultures, sometimes as protective spirits, divine messengers, or divine beings themselves. Celts and Alaskan Natives associated ravens with the creation of the world. To Pacific Northwest tribes, the raven is sacred and featured in their totem poles and other art forms.[14] The Siberian Raven God Kutcha, a powerful shaman and trickster, was seen as an ancestral figure to humans.[15]

In Scandinavian folklore, two ravens were supreme god Odin's messengers who brought him news from around the world each day. They were Hugin (thought) and Munin (memory).[16] Odin and his daughters, the Valkyries, were capable of shape-shifting into ravens.[17]

Morrigan, the Celtic goddess of the battlefield, was associated with the raven and sometimes took its form. Even Baba Yaga was rumored to turn herself into a crow at times. Crow is the companion animal of both Nephthys, the Egyptian goddess of the dead, and Dhumavati, the Hindu goddess of death.[18] In Christian, Judaic, and Islamic scriptures, ravens are mostly associated with death.

Mystified by ravens and crows and their intense blackness since ancient times, humans have projected seemingly opposite and contradictory qualities onto them. In both medieval alchemy and the Jungian interpretation of *nigredo*, blackness is a state of decomposition and stark suffering, which nevertheless holds the potential for light to emerge and gold to be formed. I particularly liked this expanded symbolic interpretation by Ted Andrews: "Black is the color of creation. It is the womb out of which the new is born. It is also the color of the night ... The crow, because of its color, was a common symbol in medieval alchemy. It represented *nigredo*, the initial state of substance, unformed but full of potential."[19]

November Garden & Landscape

"In the garden one can see the time coming for both fruition and for dying back. In the garden one is moving with rather than against the inhalations and the exhalations of greater wild Nature . . . we acknowledge that the Life/Death/Life cycle is a natural one."[20] I try to keep in mind Estés's wisdom as I prepare my garden for winter, cleaning out plant debris and covering the bare ground with cardboard and mulch to suppress weeds next spring.

By the end of the month, after many nights with temperatures in the teens, nothing seems to be alive in the open garden. Even the frost-hardy broccoli has surrendered to the cold. Even though its leaves have died down, I am hoping that I can still dig up horseradish root for fire cider, an important winter medicine. Before I close the garden gate after completing my clean-up work, I look across the fallow ground. A feeling of sadness for the garden's lost vibrancy wells up. Then another feeling emerges and quickly replaces this sense of loss: relief. My body needs rest from the physical demands of gardening, even as I miss the bounty and aliveness of the garden.

As visits to the garden become rare now, we are also cutting back on walks on our property. In Virginia, hunting season is in full progress in November. Deer, bear, and turkey, as well as smaller game like squirrel, rabbit, and quail can be hunted or "harvested" according to specific time schedules that also prescribe the type of weapons allowed (e.g. bow and arrow, muzzle loader, general firearms, and hunting with dogs).

The woodlands adjoining our property are leased to hunters who often come close to the property line or even trespass, intentionally or accidentally. Before I knew to wear orange, I had a close call while walking in the forest on a cold winter morning. As I climbed up to the top of a hill, rifle shots rang out loudly, much too close for comfort. Startled and pulse racing, I retreated downhill and back to the safety of the house.

When we do venture into the woods, we wear orange hats and talk loudly to announce our presence, supported by the warning cries of blue jays who have spotted us. The wild rose patch and hawthorn trees along the forest edge have surrendered their fruit to the animals. Under the forest trees, I discover several plants that are still very much alive: the leaves of putty-root orchid and rattlesnake plantain, both native woodland orchids; striped pipsissewa leaves surrounding a seed capsule on a brown stalk; bland partridge berries and aromatic wintergreen berries, their red color sparkling through the brown leaves carpeting the forest floor. Everything else has bedded down for winter.

When the blue jays become accustomed to our presence and stop screeching, the only sounds are the wind ebbing and lowing through the treetops and our shoes crunching the leaves underfoot. Finally, near the tiny stream that forms the boundary to the neighboring property, I find what I was looking for—witch hazel trees in bloom.

FORAGED PLANT
American Witch Hazel (*Hamamelis virginiana*)

Witch hazel, a shrub or small tree, blooms while most other plants are taking their winter break. Yellow thread-like flowers adorn its branches, at first inconspicuous among the yellowing leaves in late autumn, then in stark contrast to its bare branches. The flowers are pollinated by bees, flies, and moths on warmer days and produce a woody capsule that ejects shiny black seeds with an audible pop when they ripen during the following summer or fall. These small nutty seeds are edible and have a pistachio flavor.

Witch hazel prefers moist woods or bottomlands and is at home along the entire Eastern Seaboard, from Nova Scotia to Georgia. It grows abundantly in the understory of our oak/hickory forest. I have also found it along mountain ridges with no apparent water sources nearby.

Despite its suggestive name, witch hazel has little to do with witchcraft. The name originates from the Anglo-Saxon word *wych* or *whyche*, meaning *bend* or *pliable*.[21] However, there *is* a hint of magic here: hazelnut or witch hazel branches have long been used as dowsing or "witching" rods to locate underground water. Our well-drilling company worked with a dowser, a respected old timer, to find the best locations for our two wells. The dowser wandered across our property with witch hazel branches held out in front of him. Where the branches dipped down to the ground, the drilling rig was set up and struck water.

Witch hazel has a long history in European, Native American, and settler healing traditions because its bark, twigs, and leaves hold effective medicine that include tannins, essential oils, antioxidants, and other beneficial compounds. Witch hazel tea was used to treat internal bleeding, prevent miscarriage, and ease menstrual pain.[22] In addition, leaf infusions were used for sore throat, colds, and diarrhea.[23] A decoction of bark and leaves was applied externally to heal wounds or insect bites, soothe joint and muscle pain,[24] and for skin sores and ulcers.[25]

Contemporary applications include a decoction made from leaves and young twigs to stop bleeding and speed up healing of skin inflammation, cuts and abrasions, herpes sores, and minor burns, including sunburn. This same brew also eases itching from insect bites and poison ivy, tones the skin and tightens enlarged pores, and helps shrink varicose and spider veins including hemorrhoids. As a rinse or gargle, it can be used for mouth and throat irritations.[26,27,28]

Today's commercially available witch hazel is created through steam distillation and mixed with isopropyl alcohol for a longer shelf life. Commercial witch hazel water is the active ingredient in medicated pads, ointment, and suppositories for hemorrhoids and over-the-counter treatments for poison ivy, oak, and sumac.

I learned how to prepare witch hazel medicine from an elder Appalachian herbalist. She simmered leaves, buds, and young twigs for many hours in water, then strained out the solids. This left a brown medicinal liquid containing a much higher percentage of tannins (and other medicinal compounds) than the clear commercial liquid. My herbalist teacher told me that this concoction prevented bruising to her foot after she accidentally dropped a brick on it.

As I carefully wander around the woods this winter, I make a mental note to gather witch hazel leaves and twigs next spring for a fresh batch of medicine. For now, I delight in its yellow flowers, little sparkly streamers that offer a different kind of medicine: visual beauty and aliveness among the general dying down for winter.

Creating Sanctuary & Winter Comfort

With winter knocking on the door, I try to cultivate physical and emotional sanctuary space that invites reflection and comfort for the long months ahead. I begin by sorting through closets, dressers, and bookcases to clear out what is no longer wanted or needed—worn clothing, used books and magazines for the annual library sale, and outdated electronics that have been gathering dust. After clearing the clutter, it is much easier to create sanctuary space with warmth, color, light, and comfort in mind.

For the colors I crave, I cluster my houseplants around the great room: orchids, multicolored coleus, deep purple African violet, and maple leaf hibiscus with its orange-red tropical flowers. By midwinter, my *Phalaenopsis* orchids reliably explode with creamy white and magenta blossom magic that lasts for several months.

Our woodstove in the great room, an infrared sauna, and a comfortable bathtub become reliable spaces for bone-deep warmth during winter. I switch out a lighter blanket for a heavier one on the bed, topped by a heavy woolen throw to keep our feet toasty warm at night. Warming and nourishing drinks like home-made chai, herbal teas from the leaves and flowers I have dried throughout the growing season, turmeric milk, and hot chocolate become frequent treats. Now I crave calorie-rich foods that warm the body from the inside: bone broths, stews, root vegetables, roasts, pies, and breads. I replenish my spices and herbs for winter cooking and prepare several of my favorite winter medicines including fire cider, black cherry cough syrup, skin salves, and a mix of herbs for facial steams and tea when lungs and sinuses need relief from congestion.

To increase my light exposure, I switch on my sunlamp on gray mornings. Going for walks is easy on sunny days, more challenging on dismal, rainy days. After Thanksgiving, I often put up colorful string lights around our great room to create a cozy ambiance in the evenings. These rituals frame my sanctuary space. The Danish have a word for such winter comforts: *hygge* (pronounced hyoo-guh). Norwegians have a similar word: *koselig* (pronounced koosh-lee).[29]

When I read about people who live closer to the Arctic Circle, in northern Canada, Greenland, Scandinavia, and northern Russia, I am in awe of their ability to survive several months of twilight followed by perpetual darkness when the sun no longer rises above the horizon between mid-November and mid-January. In Finland, 85 percent of adults admit that the darkness in winter affects their mood, eating, and sleep patterns, and decreases their physical and social activities. However, only 12 percent of Finns meet the official criteria for seasonal affective disorder (SAD), which they call "kaamos-depression," after the long kaamos or polar nights. In Scandinavia, even dogs are affected by the lack of light and show symptoms of winter depression.[30]

However, researchers who studied the population of about 2,500 on Svalbard, an island cluster located between Norway and the North Pole, expressed surprise over the low levels of winter depression there. On Svalbard, people wear headlamps outside during the two-and-a-half months of polar night. Between outdoor activities, such as skiing, snowmobiling, and dog sledding, and cozy indoor spaces created with candles, blankets, woodstoves, and fireplaces, people seem to enjoy what they consider a fifth season, the polar night season.[31]

In her book *The Open-Air Life*, Linda Åkeson McGurk describes a Scandinavian lifestyle that embraces being outdoors regardless of weather or temperature. Ice-water plunges following a steamy sauna are very popular there. Municipalities all over Scandinavia cut swimming holes into frozen lakes for this purpose. Denmark, for example, has more than seventy-five winter swim clubs with registered participants known as icebreakers who regularly dip into the freezing waters.[32]

Polar-bear plunges or ice swimming have also become popular in some places in the United States. Organized events, often held on New Year's Day, can attract thousands of participants willing to brave the cold water with a quick dive or swim. As counterintuitive as it appears to a cold-avoidant creature like me, exposure to extreme cold actually strengthens the body's immune system and provides a natural high following the initial discomfort. This "cold high" is triggered by the production of noradrenaline, which regulates mood levels, increases circulation and energy, and reduces inflammation and pain in the body.[33] Nature is offering us a low-tech solution to the scarcity of sunlight in winter. While I am not drawn to a polar-bear plunge, I may test the waters, so to speak, by taking a cold shower after a steamy sauna and bundling up for more frequent walks in cold weather.

November Summary

At winter's doorstep, I consciously prepare for the loss of color, light, and warmth. There is a hint of magic in the air as we discover witch hazel's lore and medicine and the mystique of crows and ravens. These intensely black birds appear as protective spirits, divine messengers, creator figures, and harbingers of death across various cultures. In alchemy, the color black represents *nigredo*, the beginning, unformed substance that holds all future potential. This is important to keep in mind as we are going deep down into the cold season now and exploring the realm of the Crone who rules mythological wintertime.

Journaling Prompts for Self-Reflection

1. How do you feel about the coming of winter and how do you prepare for it?

2. What do you look forward to in the winter season? What do you dislike about winter?

3. How do you relate to the crone as an archetype? Estés talks about our need to reclaim the Crone's ancient wild powers including deep intuition, creative passion, and the ability to make forceful decisions. Whether you are male- or female-identified, do you see these qualities within yourself or in other people?

4. Looking at impending wintertime as an opportunity to honor the color black in an alchemical sense, what may be gathering or stirring in the darkness for you?

DECEMBER

Winter Solstice

At the end of a sullen day
frozen into gray monotones,
the clouds open to this:

> lemon zest and spring butter yellow,
> gleaming gold, ocher sand dunes,
> egg yolk orange and pumpkin spice.

Sun rays kiss
my cherry tree good night,
snuggling the snowy hill under a
somber purple cloak

> a passionate lullaby of colors
> swaying to a few breathless beats

flooding me
with certain knowing
that light will
return tomorrow.

Wintering & Winter Solstice

In addition to the darkness, another challenging aspect of winter for me is the absence of bright colors. Colors hold deep significance; they engage our senses and bring joy, wonder, and excitement. Their absence can cause lack of energy, lethargy, or depression. I remember the drab wall colors chosen in the past for government offices, military installations, prisons, and even hospitals and schools, the unappetizing muddy green or barely-there blue, the taupe of metal desks and bed frames.

In her book *Joyful*, Ingrid Fetell Lee describes the transformation of Tirana, an impoverished town in Albania, which began when the mayor had a town building painted in bright orange. Other buildings soon received a new coat of paint. Gradually, people stopped littering and began to pay their taxes. New shops and cafés opened. Within five years, the number of businesses tripled, and tax revenues increased by 600 percent. The additional revenues were used to tear down old buildings and beautify the downtown. In the early 2000s, brightly painted facades and artistic murals in the poverty-stricken *favelas* of Rio de Janeiro, Brazil, brought favorable news coverage, tourist visits, and income to these neighborhoods. Similar practices are now deployed in other cities around the world.

Pondering why color is so important to us, Lee speculated that humans evolved a refined color vision because colors often indicated food: "Over millions of generations of evolution, bright color so reliably predicted nourishment that it became intertwined with joy . . . color is an indication of the richness of our surroundings. It is an unconscious signal not only of immediate sustenance but of an environment that is capable of sustaining us over time."[1]

While I miss bright colors in winter, I still find delight and surprise in the slimmed-down winter palette, the subtle gradations of gray lichen on tree bark, muted greens of conifers, browns of sedges and barren patches of soil. Now, the structural and textural elements in nature command attention: the trees' winter bones, their skeletal trunks and branches, their branching patterns resembling the fractal lines of a river delta on a map. Long tree shadows paint intriguing patterns across the landscape, even more pronounced after snowfall.

Winter solstice occurs on December 21 or 22 in the northern hemisphere. The shortest day of the year has held deep significance since ancient times, when that day represented a turning point, the rebirth of the sun and the beginning of a new year. Over twenty major spiritual traditions around the world celebrate this special time. Since the sun was identified as a masculine deity by some ancient cultures, winter solstice has sometimes been considered the return of the divine masculine.[2]

Magnificent stone, wood, and earthen structures, such as Newgrange in Ireland, the Serpent Mound in Ohio, and the Cahokia Mounds historic site (Woodhenge) in Illinois mark the summer and winter solstices. These ancient masterpieces of stone and earth allowed the sun to illuminate recessed chambers at Newgrange or precisely align various points of human-made structures like the temple pyramids at Woodhenge during solstice times. It is speculated that, in addition to determining the summer and winter solstices, Woodhenge also may have served as a solar calendar for planting crops and scheduling religious ceremonies. We no longer know the exact nature of rituals and celebrations conducted in such places. However, there is no doubt that the solstices were so intrinsically important to our ancestors that they warranted the creation of such monumental spaces.[3]

Throughout Europe, solstice customs and rituals have prevailed through the ages. In his book *Wilder Mann: The Image of the Savage*, French photographer Charles Fréger captured stunning photographs of tribal traditions from eighteen European countries that include people masquerading in street parades to mark various phases of winter. Their costumes, complete with often frightening masks, are constructed from materials such as animal pelts, antlers, horns, bones, tree branches, straw, and bells designed to turn humans into wild animals or devils. Depending on the country, these parades are held at different times during winter, beginning in December and extending into March.[4]

Masqueraders in devil costumes usher in the Christmas season in early December in Austria, Germany, and many eastern European countries. This is known as *Krampusnacht* (Night of the Krampus) and is now also celebrated in communities in

Canada and in cities like Seattle and Philadelphia in the United States. Krampus tends to be popular in the alpine regions of Germany,[5] while Knecht Ruprecht is a more familiar figure in other parts of Germany (and virtually unknown elsewhere)[6] and Zwarte Piet (Black Peter) is the companion of St. Nicholas, or Santa Claus, in the Netherlands.[7] While St. Nicholas has the pleasant task of rewarding "good" children with sweets, his fearsome companion doles out punishment to those children who have been "bad." Krampus is depicted as part goat and part human with at least one cloven hoof.[8,9] It is often speculated that Krampus originated in pre-Christian times, and I suspect that he may have been the pagan horned god himself who was later transformed into a devil figure by the Christian church.

In the Americas, winter solstice ceremonies and celebrations are observed by North American tribes in December, while in Central and South America, they are held in June, the beginning of winter in the southern hemisphere. The Zuni Pueblo organizes the annual Shalako festival, which is not open to the non-native public. Here, too, costumes play an important role: men dress up in bird costumes to honor bird deities whose blessings are believed to be beneficial not only to the Zuni Pueblo tribe but to the entire world community. The Blackfeet tribe in Montana observes the winter solstice and the "return" of the sun, called "Naatosi," with games, drumming, and dances.[10]

Deer & Reindeer Goddesses

Elen, the Deer Mother or deer goddess of the British Isles, is often depicted as a beautiful antlered woman. She is also called Elen of the Ways, or Goddess of the Ancient Tracks. The Ways refer to the deer paths crisscrossing the British Isles, said to be superimposed on energy pathways along the earth's surface.[11] Many early settlements and sacred sites were built over subterranean wells through which these energy lines were believed to be passing.[12] While only scant historical evidence of the deer goddess remains in the British Isles, there are extensive archeological discoveries in Scandinavia, Siberia, and Central Asia, where thousands of deer and reindeer images on rock carvings, paintings, and monolithic stone monuments attest to her pervasive spiritual importance from the Neolithic era to the Bronze Age.[13]

In the arctic regions, indigenous tribes depended on reindeer for all aspects of their lives, as a food source, skins for clothing and shelter, and as a means of transportation.[14] Not surprisingly, the deer/reindeer goddess was the personification of the Great Earth Mother in the circumpolar regions. Since Neolithic times, she has been connected to fertility and motherhood and ruled over the return of the sun at the winter solstice. Shamans wore antlers in ceremonies invoking the goddess. Antlers decorated shrines and altars. Deer and reindeer images were carved into standing stones and rock walls and decorated clothing, jewelry, and drums discovered in ancient Sami and Siberian burial sites.[15] The antlered ones were held in such high esteem that people even tattooed them on their bodies. A 2,500-year-old mummy, surprisingly well preserved in the Siberian permafrost, was identified as a woman of high status who died in her twenties. Her skin was covered with extensive tattoos including a deer-like animal with magnificent antlers.[16]

A related Nordic goddess revered in Latvia and Lithuania is the sun goddess Saule who flies across the sky in a sleigh pulled by antlered reindeer (or sometimes horses). Saule throws presents into people's chimneys in the form of small pieces of amber. The golden-yellow color of amber symbolizes the sun.[17] She is especially revered by women, as she bestows fertility and healing. Saule means *sun*, and she rules over all other celestial beings. The winter solstice period into early January is dedicated to Saule.[18]

The Sami, indigenous people of northern Scandinavia and parts of Russia, venerate Beaivi and her daughter, Beaivi-nieda. This sun goddess, like Saule and the Siberian reindeer goddess, is connected to motherhood and fertility. She and her daughter were often depicted within a frame of reindeer antlers.[19]

In his documentary *The Reindeer People*, anthropologist Dr. Hamid Sardar-Afkhami follows a group of the nomadic Dukha people in northern Mongolia. The Dukha have domesticated reindeer and rely on their herd for milk, cheese, and fur. Only a few dozen families remain who live this ancient lifestyle. The female leader of the Dukha is Tsuyan, a ninety-six-year-old shaman. In the film synopsis, she is described as "the link between the healing songs of the forest ancestors, her people, and their reindeer. She is the centerpiece of an extraordinary adventure that unites people and animals in one of the wildest regions of Mongolia, where people still live and hunt in a forest dominated by supernatural beings." Tsuyan and her small community may represent one of the few surviving human links to the ancient reindeer goddess.[20,21]

Deer

White-tailed deer and reindeer, along with mule deer, moose, and elk are all members of the deer family. As far as I know, there are no reindeer in the wild in Virginia. We do have plenty of white-tailed deer. They habitually traverse the same routes that have turned into narrow foot paths on our property.

Once almost extinct due to overhunting, whitetail deer (*Odocoileus virginianus*) have become the most numerous of the large mammals in North America. They inhabit most of southern Canada and mainland United States and range throughout Central America into Bolivia, South America. As highly adaptable creatures, they thrive in the woodlands of northern Maine, the swamps of Florida, and even the cactus deserts of Texas and Mexico.[22]

The white-tailed deer received its name from the white underside of its tail, which it raises like a flag when running away from a perceived threat. While deer have good eyesight and hearing, they rely primarily on their sense of smell to detect the presence of predators. They use scent glands on their hooves and legs to communicate with other deer, especially during rutting season.[23]

Their reddish-brown coat turns gray in winter. Deer fawns are known for their white spots, which fade by the first winter of their life. Bucks start growing new antlers with spring's increasing daylight and shed them in late winter. As light decreases in autumn, bucks begin to shed the skin (velvet) on the antlers, which also triggers increased testosterone production, just in time for rutting season.[24] Bucks fight each other for the right to mate with a particular female. In our area, I've only seen young stags clashing their antlers. Older males with their magnificent antlers are rare. The longevity required to develop such a grand rack is likely cut short by hunters who take them down prematurely.

Does give birth to their young in late spring and leave them behind while they find food for themselves. The fawns' spotted coat serves as perfect camouflage in the dabbled shade of the forest's edge or in tall grasses. They remain motionless, making it harder for predators to find them. However, there is only so much closeness a fawn can tolerate and stay still. I once discovered a blue-eyed fawn bedded down in the grass just outside my garden. When I approached it wondering whether it was injured, it stopped playing dead and ran away, bleating loudly like a baby goat.

While I was familiar with the deer's warning sound, a loud snort, I was entirely unprepared for this enchanting scene: One summer evening, I watched a deer with her two babies by a small pond. The fawns chased each other around the pond bleating with excitement, just like human children shrieking with delight. Unperturbed by her children's antics, Mama Deer continued grazing in her dignified manner.

White-tailed deer are well-adapted herbivores who eat grasses, leaves, and berries in spring and summer. I love seeing deer balance on their hind legs to pick apples or wild cherries from low-hanging branches. In autumn, they feed on fruit, nuts, and acorns to fatten up for winter when they resort to eating tree bark, twigs, and buds, along with any grasses they can find under the snow cover.[25]

Farmers and gardeners have reason to dislike deer when they eat their field crops and cause damage to fruit trees and ornamental shrubs. In many urban and suburban areas, deer have become overabundant because of a lack of natural predators. Vehicle collisions kill many deer each year and can result in serious injury to the human occupants of the vehicles.

Here, in the Highlands of Virginia, bobcat, bear, coyote, and humans are major deer predators. Whitetail deer are hunted for meat and sport. In the past, early settlers and Native Americans turned deer hides into clothing and other useful products. Now, deer hides frequently end up in roadside dumpsters during hunting season. Antlered heads, on the other hand, are often prepared by taxidermists for mounting on the walls of barns, hunting lodges, even living rooms as a proud display of hunting prowess. The stuffed heads with their glassy eyes always seem a bit spooky to me, as if they might still be alive.

December Garden & Landscape

A single tree holds onto its leaves into early December. Glowing golden orange in the setting sun, it is the last holdout among all deciduous trees on our property. It eventually surrenders its leaves. All that remains of the deciduous trees now are their skeleton trunks and branches. While I miss the leaves, their whispers and rustlings, I am intrigued by the newly revealed structures of trees, the unique shapes of bare branches that now expose a covering of lichen, a small patch of moss, or a tiny vine beginning to climb. Without leaves, there is more spaciousness and transparency. Through the trees' winter bones, I spot houses that I had not seen before, along with landscape features like ridges and rock clusters that are camouflaged during the green season. Birds have fewer places to hide, and abandoned nests are exposed.

Now the evergreen conifers receive the attention their deciduous neighbors took from them. When I walk into a grouping of five tall pine trees on our property, I notice the stillness there. These trees buffer the flow of air and sound, offering safe shelter. Old pine needles are matted down in this area, surely a resting place for deer. I like to clip a few branches from these pines and arrange them in a large vase interspersed with stalks of orange Chinese lanterns or red rosehips. This simple year-end practice spreads the resinous fragrance of pine through the house, and its dark green presence feels reassuring and grounding.

FORAGED PLANT
Pine (*Pinus species*)

Conifers, the iconic evergreen trees, are some of the oldest woody plants on earth. They have been around as a species for over two hundred million years, much longer than humans. A bristlecone pine in the White Mountains of California named Methuselah is one of the world's oldest living trees, estimated to be over 4,600 years old.[26]

In the United States, conifer species include bald cypress, cedar, Douglas fir, true fir, hemlock, larch, pine, redwood, and spruce. Worldwide, there are over six hundred species.[27] The conifers growing on our Virginia property are primarily Eastern white pine (*Pinus strobus*) and a small stand of hemlock trees (*Tsuga canadensis*) that, so far, has escaped the hemlock woolly adelgid, a destructive insect pest responsible for massive die-offs of these beautiful evergreens in the eastern US and Canada.

I like to visit the groves of old-growth virgin spruce trees in nearby West Virginia, which miraculously survived the surrounding clear-cutting frenzies. Here, I inhale the fresh resin scent and soak in the deep quiet that settles among these grandmother trees. Moss-covered hillocks soften the ground beneath the trees, dotted occasionally by a few mushrooms. Snow cover creates fairy-tale forest scenes reminding me of the Black Forest, the magic-infused woodlands of my childhood.

Pine is an extremely useful tree. It provides lumber for construction and wood pulp for paper products. The ceiling panels and window frames in our house, along with bookshelves and some cabinetry are made from white pine. Pinecones and boughs are popular for crafting wreaths and other wintertime decorations. Pine needles can be woven into baskets, a craft originally perfected by Native Americans.

All parts of a pine tree—needles, nuts, inner bark, resin, and pollen—lend themselves to culinary and medicinal uses. Many Native Americans traditionally used pine to treat cold and flu symptoms, clean wounds, and ease rheumatism.[28] Modern medical science has confirmed pine's many healing qualities that include pain-reducing, anti-inflammatory, antimicrobial, mucus-suppressing, wound-healing, and lymph- and immune-support functions.[29]

Pine seeds, also called pine nuts or piñons, are in demand for cooking and baking and offer health and nutritional benefits, including antioxidants, vitamins, and minerals.

Pine needles contain high amounts of vitamins A and C. The tender young needles can be lightly steamed and sprinkled on meals. In winter, pine needles make a nourishing tea by themselves or paired with warming spices and herbs like cinnamon, thyme, or rosemary. Pine needle tea is also a traditional remedy for fever, cough, cold, allergies, and urinary tract and sinus infections.[30] Tea is easily prepared by simmering a small handful of pine needles in water for twenty minutes. Strain, add honey, and sip while hot.

Pine's white inner bark, the cambium, is located just beneath the coarse outer bark. This soft inner bark is edible, either raw or dried and ground into a flour substitute. Like pine needles, it is high in vitamins A and C and served as survival food for indigenous people when other foods ran scarce in winter.[31] Cambium can also be used medicinally as an antimicrobial wash or wound cover. Infused in bathwater, it helps ease muscle aches and pains. As a tea, it becomes a remedy for coughs and colds, similar to pine needle tea.[32]

Pine resin, or pitch, is formed by the tree as protection against pathogens after an injury to its trunk or branches.[33] This sticky substance has first-aid uses as an antimicrobial wound dressing and for drawing out splinters from the skin or toxins from insect bites. Pine resin salve soothes muscle aches and decreases joint inflammation.[34,35,36]

To identify pine, look for the familiar pinecones and bundles of two to five needles held together by a tiny papery sheath at the base. While spruce and fir are easily confused with pine, they can be used interchangeably for medicinal and culinary purposes. However, the yew tree has poisonous needles. Fortunately, its red fleshy fruit helps to differentiate yew from the cone-bearing conifers. Pine needles and pine bark can irritate the kidneys of some individuals. Pine resin should only be used externally by lay people, and all pine products should be avoided during pregnancy.[37]

Honoring Liminal Space

For a week or two after Christmas, I feel a bit unmoored, unsure of what day it is. There are no appointments, no social commitments. Time slows down. In fact, this is the "catch-up" time between the lunar calendar that consists of 354 days and the solar calendar that includes 365 days (366 in a leap year). The difference between these calendars leaves eleven days or twelve nights at the end of the year creating a "time between times," which is often experienced as liminal space (derived from the Latin word for threshold, *limen*).[38]

This frequently windy and unsettled time gave rise to legends of the Wild Hunt (*Wilde Jagd*) in the Germanic and Scandinavian regions of Europe. Supernatural beings on horseback, sometimes seen as evil spirits, rode through the night skies, led by

Odin, Frau Holle, or Frau Perchta, depending on geography and culture. Encountering such a wild hunt could result in punishment or even death; best to remain inside, by the warm hearth.[39]

In the Germanic regions, the days between the winter solstice and January 6 (Epiphany) are known as *Rauhnächte* (rough nights or smoky nights). People purified house and barn with the smoke from herbs and resins, such as frankincense, myrrh, juniper, and pine. Ritual smudging, fireworks, banging on pots, and ringing of church bells were customary year-end activities to chase evil spirits away. Meat and cake were left outside for the leaders of the Wild Hunt. During these *Rauhnächte*, rest became mandatory: no more spinning, laundry, or other housework, no more gambling or card playing. In pre-Christian times, a boar was sacrificed to Freya, a Nordic goddess. Perhaps this is the reason why Germans still give each other pink marzipan pigs as good luck charms for the new year.[40]

These transitional days at the end of the year were a time not only for protection but also for divination. Families practiced lead or wax pouring (*Bleigießen* or *Wachsgießen*) by melting lead or wax in a spoon heated over a flame, then dripping it into a bowl of cold water. The melted substance hardened into shapes that were carefully inspected as omens for the future.[41]

My favorite things to do between winter solstice and the first few weeks of the new year are not so different from these old customs that serve to let go of the energies of the old year and envision the year to come. I often keep a gratitude jar and drop in slips of paper with scribbled examples of what I was grateful for throughout the year. At year's end, I review and savor the good things that came my way, from the small everyday delights and luxuries, such as good fair-trade coffee and eggs from free-range chickens, to the great privilege of living my life just the way I choose it. Reading through the contents of my gratitude jar, the year gleams in the warmth of these moments captured on random slips of paper; my life feels abundant, my heart feels full, and I am ready for the coming year.

I enjoy creating a collage of images salvaged from magazines, calendars, and junk mail. The pictures create a synergistic composite of the qualities and things I want to manifest, a practice similar to lead pouring but far less toxic.

Now is a good time to dim or switch off electrical lights and to gaze into the flames of the fireplace or candles, to peer at star constellations in the dark night sky, to listen to the winds of change. Both candle and firelight emit infrared light that does not disturb our circadian and sleep rhythms. The flames invite daydreaming and a quieting of mind and heart. Faces soften and become more beautiful, appearing to glow from within. Voices become quieter, conversational pauses stretch out longer, and we are drawn to sharing stories from the heart. At dusk, I watch the vanishing of daylight, intrigued by how known objects turn into ambiguous shapes, how a dark spot in the grass or a mass in a tree now looks like a bear or a wildcat, or something else that wasn't there before. Peering into the darkening, I feel unexpectedly at ease in this ambiguous, liminal space and trust that whatever lies beyond the threshold is already taking shape and positioning itself along the path of the new year.

December Summary

Winter brings remnants of Northern ancestral traditions, holdovers from times when winter forces could easily kill those who were unprepared. Even in our more buffered and comfortable lifestyles, a blizzard will quickly remind us of our vulnerability to the harsh power of winter. The deer/reindeer goddess was the personification of the Great Earth Mother for those who depended on these animals for survival. In our times, deer are often considered a nuisance. Killed for sport, sometimes for meat, their hides discarded as trash, deer are barely a shadowy remainder of their once lifesaving and honored role.

The absence of colors and darkening of days invite us to tune in to winter's subtleties, to pay close attention to gradations of sensation and lived experience. We may choose to observe the liminal transition into the new year with contemplative practices, ever deepening the theme of the month, wintering.

Journaling Prompts for Self-Reflection

1. Looking back on this past year, what do you want to leave behind and what do you want to take with you into the coming year?

2. How can you listen deeply into the winter silence? What is the silence telling you?

3. How do you connect with your inner knowing?

4. What physical activity keeps your body moving even in the depth of winter?

5. What kind of divination are you familiar with (some examples include tarot cards; collage making; free-association journaling; opening a book randomly to read a paragraph; a waking dream; or noticing an animal, plant or other object you come across to examine its personal symbolism for you)? Would one or more of these practices guide you more deeply into questions #2 and #3?

ENDNOTES

Introduction

1 Hannah Ritchie, Veronika Samborska, and Max Roser, "Urbanization," *Our World in Data*, February 2024, https://ourworldindata.org/urbanization.

January

1 David Whyte, *Consolations: The Solace, Nourishment and Underlying Meaning of Everyday Words* (Langley, WA: Many Rivers Press, 2015), 115.

2 Tamra Andrews, *A Dictionary of Nature Myths* (New York: Oxford Press, 1998), 76.

3 Andrews, *Myths*, 183.

4 Andrews, *Myths*, 76.

5 Andrews, *Myths*, 183–184.

6 Andrews, *Myths*, 76.

7 Andrews, *Myths*, 184.

8 Hope B. Werness, *The Continuum Encyclopedia of Animal Symbolism in Art* (New York: Continuum, 2004).

9 Jamie Sams and David Carson, *Medicine Cards* (New York: St. Martin's, 1999), 57.

10 Elizabeth V. Spelman, *Repair: The Impulse to Restore in a Fragile World* (Boston: Beacon, 2002), 5.

11 The Daily Difference Newsletter, "News from France in the Fight against Fashion Waste," *The Carbon Almanac*, June 28, 2023, https:/ /thecarbonalmanac.org/news-from-france-in-the-fight-against -fashion-waste/.

12 Kelly Richman-Abdou, "Kintsugi: The Centuries-Old Art of Repairing Broken Pottery with Gold," *My Modern Met*, March 5, 2022, https:/ /mymodernmet.com/kintsugi-kintsukuroi/.

13 Nina and Sonya Montenegro, *Mending Life: A Handbook for Repairing Clothes and Hearts* (Seattle: Sasquatch Books, 2020).

February

1 Martin Byrne, *The Fr. Michael O'Flanagan History and Heritage Center*, "The Hill of Tara," accessed October 28, 2023, http://www.carrowkeel .com/sites/tara/.

2 "Bridget's Life, Wells and Customs," *Tara Celebrations*, January 31, 2019, https://www.taracelebrations.org/celebrations/imbolc/bridgets-life -wells-and-customs.

3 Danielle P. Olson, "Imbolc & the Rites of Women: The Midwinter Festival of Lights," *Gather Victoria*, December 15, 2017, https:/ /gathervictoria.com/2017/12/15/sympathetic-magic-and-the -midwinter-festival-of-lights/.

4 Olson, "Imbolc & the Rites of Women."

5 Glenda C. Booth, "Virginia's Most Mysterious Birds," *Virginia Department of Wildlife Resources*, accessed October 29, 2023, https://dwr .virginia.gov/blog/virginias-most-mysterious-birds/.

6 Monica Sjöö and Barbara Mor, *The Great Cosmic Mother: Rediscovering the Religion of the Earth* (San Francisco: Harper/Collins, 1991), 96–98.

7 Michael Everson, "Tenacity in Religion, Myth, and Folklore: the Neolithic Goddess of Old Europe Preserved in a Non-Indo-European Setting," *Journal of Indo-European Studies* 17 nos. 3 & 4 (Fall/Winter 1989), 277–95.

8 Kitty Fields, "Owl Goddesses," *Otherworldly Oracle*, August 20, 2019, https://otherworldlyoracle.com/owl-Goddesses/.

9 Thunderbird, "Owl Medicine, the Sacred Medicine of Deception, always asking, Hoo, Hoo?" *Doowans*, October 24, 2013, https://doowans.com /owl-medicine/.

10 Nancy Blair, *Amulets of the Goddess* (Oakland, CA: Wingbow Press, 1993), 125.

11 Fields, "Owl Goddesses."

12 Annette Naber, "Inside the Maple-Sugar Camps—Sweet Winter Harvest," *Beauty Along the Road*, March 21, 2014, https://beautyalongtheroad .wordpress.com/2014/03/21/inside-the-maple-sugar-camps-sweet -winter-harvest/.

13 Anne-Marie Bonneau, "23 Simple Ways to Reduce Planet-Heating Wasted Food," *The Zero-Waste Chef*, January 10, 2019, https://zerowastechef .com/2019/01/10/23-ways-to-end-planet-heating-food-waste/.

14 Bonneau, "23 Simple Ways."

15 Tamar Adler, *An Everlasting Meal: Cooking with Economy and Grace* (New York: Scribner, 2011), 53.

16 Adler, *An Everlasting Meal*, 57.

17 Adler, *An Everlasting Meal*, 58.

18 Bonneau, "Vegetable Broth Recipe Ideas," *The Zero-Waste Chef*, January 28, 2021, https://zerowastechef.com/2021/01/28/vegetable -broth-recipe-ideas/.

19 Bonneau, "15 Creative Uses for Food Scraps, *The Zero- Waste Chef*, May 2, 2018, https://zerowastechef. com/2018/05/02/15-creative-uses-food-scraps/.

March

1 Jon Young, *What the Robin Knows: How Birds Reveal the Secrets of the Natural World* (Boston: Houghton Mifflin Harcourt, 2012).

2 Tamra Andrews, *A Dictionary of Nature Myths* (New York: Oxford Press, 1998), 74.

3 Andrews, *Myths*, 174–175.

4 Andrews, *Myths*, 175.

5 "USDA Wildlife Services Posts FY2020 Data on Management Actions and Funding Sources," U.S. Department of Agriculture Animal and Plant Health Inspection Service, March 17, 2021, https://www.aphis.usda.gov/aphis/newsroom/stakeholder-info/stakeholder-messages/wildlife-damage-news/ws-post-pdr.

6 "Native American Coyote Mythology," *Native Languages of the Americas: Preserving and Promoting American Indian Languages*, accessed November 7, 2023, http://www.native-languages.org/legends-coyote.htm.

7 James Deutsch, "Loki's Place in Trickster Mythology," *Smithsonian*, June 9, 2021, https://getpocket.com/explore/item/loki-s-place-in-trickster-mythology?utm_source=pocket-newtab.

8 "Native American Coyote Mythology," *Native Languages of the Americas: Preserving and Promoting American Indian Languages*, accessed June 11, 2024, https://www.native-languages.org/legends-coyote.htm.

9 Susan Patterson, "4 Reasons To Go & Find Purple Dead-Nettle," *Natural Living Ideas*, April 2, 2020, https://www.naturallivingideas.com/purple-dead-nettle/?utm_source=facebook&utm_medium=social&utm_campaign=social-pug&fbclid=IwAR3SIjALTo8D3gFJZ8IZdKVg12a8h-S-EhNaX7nBk8Uf_txLbYWlga_drdg.

10 Jan Berry, "How to Make Purple Dead Nettle Salve," *The Nerdy Farmwife*, accessed November 7, 2023, https://thenerdyfarmwife.com/purple-dead-nettle-salve/.

11 Berry, "How to Make Purple Dead Nettle Salve."

12 Danielle P. Olson, "Spring Cleaning! The Magical Powers of the Besom," *Gather Victoria*, March 20, 2019, https://gathervictoria.com/2019/03/20/spring-cleaning-the-magical-besom/.

13 Christina Caron, "This Year, Try Spring Cleaning Your Brain," *The New York Times*, March 14, 2022, https://www.nytimes.com/2022/03/14/well/mind/stress-anxiety-mind.html?referringSource=articleShare.

14 Parker J. Palmer, "Spring is Mud and Miracle," *On Being*, March 29, 2016, https://onbeing.org/blog/spring-is-mud-and-miracle/?fbclid=IwAR3vkoQxfe1IIXu4fCbTbLPxWWpXsxVecOxOk3ouyHQPJoJqS6uQqK_PyFw.

April

1 "What Is Hildegard's Viriditas?" *Healthy Hildegard*, accessed November 11, 2023, https://www.healthyhildegard.com/hildegards-viriditas/.

2 "Ostara/Spring Equinox/Vernal Equinox March 21–22," *The Goddess and the Green Man*, July 20, 2022, https://www.goddessandgreenman.co.uk/blog/ostara-spring-equinox-21-march.

3 "Ēostre," *Wikipedia*, accessed November 11, 2023, https://en.wikipedia
   .org/wiki/%C4%92ostre.

4 "Ēostre," *Wikipedia*.

5 Krystal D'Costa, "Beyond Ishtar: The Tradition of Eggs at Easter,"
   Scientific American, March 31, 2013, https://blogs.scientificamerican
   .com/anthropology-in-practice/beyond-ishtar-the-tradition-of-eggs
   -at-easter/.

6 D'Costa, "Beyond Ishtar."

7 Andrew Amelinckx, "Five Differences Between Rabbits and Hares,"
   Modern Farmer, March 25, 2017, https://modernfarmer.com/2017/03
   /five-differences-rabbits-hares/.

8 "Ostara/Spring Equinox," *The Goddess and the Green Man*.

9 David Cunningham, "African American folktale," *Britannica*, accessed
   November 11, 2023, https://www.britannica.com/art/African-American
   -folktale#ref1222868.

10 Juliet Blankespoor, *The Healing Garden: Cultivating & Handcrafting
   Herbal Remedies* (New York: Mariner Books, 2022), 247–250.

11 Blankespoor, *The Healing Garden*, 250.

12 "Chlorophyll," *National Geographic*, accessed November 13, 2023,
   https://www.nationalgeographic.org/encyclopedia/chlorophyll/.

13 "Photosynthesis," *National Geographic*, accessed November 13, 2023,
   https://education.nationalgeographic.org/resource/photosynthesis/
   ?utm_source=BibblioRCM_Row.

14 "Dandelion greens, raw," USDA, *Agricultural Research Service*, Food Data
   Central, accessed November 13, 2023, https://fdc.nal.usda.gov/fdc-app
   .html#/food-details/169226/nutrients.

15 James A. Duke, Ph.D., *The Green Pharmacy* (Emmaus, PA: Rodale
   Press, 1997).

16 Danielle P. Olson, "Wild Spring Greens: A Superfood Recipe
   Round-up!" *Gather Victoria*, March 19, 2020, https://gathervictoria
   .com2020/03/19/wild-spring-greens-a-superfood-recipe-round-up/.

17 Jo Robinson, *Eating On The Wild Side: The Missing Link to Optimum
   Health* (New York: Little, Brown, 2013), 9.

18 Robinson, *Eating On The Wild Side*, 10.

19 Robinson, *Eating on the Wild Side*, 4.

20 Holly McCord, RD, "Your Guide To The Glycemic Index," *Prevention*,
   November 3, 2011 https://www.prevention.com/food-nutrition
   /healthy-eating/a20428261/glycemic-index-and-blood-sugar-levels/.

21 Centers for Disease Control and Prevention, "State Indicator Report on
   Fruits and Vegetables, 2018," January 7, 2022 https://www.cdc
   .gov/nutrition/data-statistics/2018-state-indicator-report-fruits
   -vegetables.html.

22 Monica "Mo" Wilde, email message to author, April 5, 2024.

23 Timothy Lee Scott, *Invasive Plant Medicine: The Ecological Benefits and Healing Abilities of Invasives* (Rochester, VT: Healing Arts Press, 2010).

24 Douglas W. Tallamy, *Bringing Nature Home: How You Can Sustain Wildlife with Native Plants* (Portland, OR: Timber Press, 2013).

May

1 Barbara Walker, *The Woman's Dictionary of Symbols and Sacred Objects* (San Francisco: Harper Collins, 1988), 25.

2 Judika Illes, *The Encyclopedia of Spirits: The Ultimate Guide to the Magic of Fairies, Genies, Demons, Ghosts, Gods & Goddesses* (New York: Harper One, 2009), 454.

3 "Beltane April 30–May 1," *The Goddess and the Greenman*, July 25, 2022, https://www.goddessandgreenman.co.uk.

4 "Khidr," *Wikipedia*, accessed November 15, 2023, https://en.wikipedia.org/wiki/Khidr.

5 Tamra Andrews, *A Dictionary of Nature Myths* (New York: Oxford Press, 1998).

6 Illes, *Encyclopedia of Spirits*, 412.

7 Illes, *Encyclopedia of Spirits*, 321.

8 "The Green Man," *Misfits and Heroes*, August 12, 2022, https://misfitsandheroes.wordpress.com/2022/08/12/_trashed.

9 "The Green Man," *Misfits and Heroes*.

10 "The Hubertus Legend-the Story behind the Stag," *Jägermeister Global Website*, accessed November 15, 2023, https://www.jagermeister.com/en/jaegermeister-tales/the-hubertus-legend-a-stag-night-to-remember.

11 Singing Head, "Basajaun, the Lord of the Forest," *Sareoso*, June 23, 2020, https://sareoso.wordpress.com/2020/06/23/basajaun-the-lord-of-the-forest/.

12 Illes, *Encyclopedia of Spirits*, 451.

13 Illes, *Encyclopedia of Spirits*, 873–874.

14 Annette Naber, "Hummingbirds: Avian Jewels," *The Beauty Along the Road*, August 20, 2014, https://beautyalongtheroad.wordpress.com/2014/08/20/hummingbirds-avian-jewels/.

15 "Native American Hummingbird Mythology", *Native Languages*, accessed November 15, 2023, http://www.native-languages.org/legends-hummingbird.htm.

16 "Urtica dioica (Urticaceae)," USDA Agricultural Research Service, *Dr. Duke's Phytochemical and Ethnobotanical Databases*, accessed June 12, 2024, https://phytochem.nal.usda.gov/phytochem/plants/show/6871#page-1.

17 Rosalee de la Forêt & Emily Han, *Wild Remedies: How to Forage Healing Foods and Craft your Own Herbal Medicine* (New York: Hay House, 2020), 115–119.

18 Steven Horne, "Stinging Nettles: Nourishing Food and Strengthening Medicine," *Steven Horne's Newsletter*, June 23, 2020.

June

1 Diane Ackerman, *A Natural History of the Senses* (New York: Vintage, 1991), 309.

2 Michael J. Cohen, *Reconnecting With Nature* (Lakeville, MN: Ecopress, 2007).

3 Judika Illes, *The Encyclopedia of Spirits: The Ultimate Guide to the Magic of Fairies, Genies, Demons, Ghosts, Gods & Goddesses* (New York: Harper One, 2009), 414.

4 Illes, *Encyclopedia of Spirits*, 415.

5 Ed Whelan, "Flora, Goddess of Spring, and Her Festival Floralia," *Classical Wisdom*, April 2, 2021, https://classicalwisdom.com/mythology/gods/flora-goddess-of-spring-and-her-festival-floralia/.

6 "Litha/Summer Solstice June 21," *The Goddess and the Green Man*, July 26, 2022, https://www.goddessandgreenman.co.uk/blog/litha-summer-solstice-june-21.

7 Tamra Andrews, *Dictionary of Nature Myths* (Oxford: Oxford Press, 1998), 22.

8 Andrews, *Nature Myths*, 127.

9 "About Mountain Lions," *Mountain Lion Foundation*, accessed November 28, 2023, https://mountainlion.org/about-mountain-lions/.

10 "Eastern Cougar (Puma)," *Virginia Department of Wildlife Resources*, accessed August 18, 2023, https://dwr.virginia.gov/wildlife/information/eastern-cougar-puma/.

11 "Native American Cougar Mythology," *Native Languages*, accessed November 28, 2023, https://www.native-languages.org/legends-cougar.htm.

12 Kristen M.Stanton, "Cougar Meanings, Symbolism & Spirit Animal," *Uniguide*, August 12, 2023, https://www.uniguide.com/cougar-meaning-symbolism-spirit-animal.

13 John Kallas. *Edible Wild Plants: Wild Foods from Dirt to Plate* (Layton, UT: Gibbs Smith, 2010), 68–69.

14 "How to Use Lambsquarter from Root to Plant to Seed," *Chelsea Green Publishing*, accessed November 29, 2023, https://www.chelseagreen.com/2023/use-lambsquarter-from-root-to-seed/.

15 Juliet Blankespoor, "Edible and Medicinal Wild Herbs" (Online Foraging Course), *Chestnut School of Herbal Medicine*, accessed November 28, 2023, https://courses.chestnutherbs.com.

16 Kallas, *Edible Wild Plants*, 72.

17 Hugh Brody, *The Other Side of Eden: Hunters, Farmers, and the Shaping of the World* (New York: North Point Press, 2000).

18 Brody, *The Other Side of Eden*.

19 Mo Wilde, *The Wilderness Cure: Ancient Wisdom in a Modern World* (New York: Simon & Schuster, 2022).

20 Jessica Carew Kraft, *Why We Need to Be Wild: One Woman's Quest for Ancient Human Answers to 21st Century Problems* (Naperville, IL: Sourcebooks, 2023).

21 Brianne Dela Cruz, "15 Ways to Rewild Yourself," *Gather and Grow*, Aug 2, 2020, https://gatherandgrow.com/blog/15-ways-to-rewild-yourself/2020/8/2.

22 Dela Cruz, "15 Ways to Rewild Yourself."

July

1 Rainer Maria Rilke, *Letters of Rainer Maria Rilke, 1892–1910* (New York: W. W. Norton, 1969).

2 Tamra Andrews, *Dictionary of Nature Myths* (Oxford: Oxford Press, 1998), 192–193.

3 Andrews, *Nature Myths*, 177.

4 Andrews, *Nature Myths*, 90.

5 Andrews, *Nature Myths*, 127.

6 Andrews, *Nature Myths*, 193.

7 Christopher Minster, "All About the Inca Sun God," *ThoughtCo*, May 30, 2019, https://www.thoughtco.com/inti-the-inca-sun-god-2136316.

8 "Inti Raymi: The Most Important Festival of the Inca Empire," *Peru Travel*, July 9, 2020. https://www.peru.travel/en/masperu/inti-raymi-the-most-important-festival-of-the-inca-empire.

9 Frances Wood and Bob Sundstrom, "The Wild Turkey—One Well-Traveled Bird," *BirdNote*, November 28, 2019, https://www.birdnote.org/listen/shows/wild-turkey-one-well-traveled-bird.

10 Cyler Conrad, "Five Ways Native American Communities Honor Turkeys," *Sapiens.org*, November 23, 2021, https://www.sapiens.org/archaeology/native-americans-turkey/.

11 Sarah Zielinski, "14 Fun Facts About Turkeys," *Smithsonian* (November 15, 2012), https://www.smithsonianmag.com/science-nature/14-fun-facts-about-turkeys-665520/.

12 Zielinski, *Smithsonian*.

13 Zielinski, *Smithsonian*.

14 Zielinski, *Smithsonian*.

15 Mike Weilbacher, "Wild Turkeys: Of Wingmen and Bands of Brothers," *Schuylkill Center*, November 21, 2012, https://www.schuylkillcenter.org/news/wild-turkeys-of-wingmen-and-bands-of-brothers/.

16 Erin Blakemore, "Turkeys Were Once Worshipped Like Gods," *History*, November 7, 2023, https://www.history.com/news/turkey-worship-maya.

17 "Native American Turkey Mythology," *Native Languages* (accessed December 2, 2023), http://www.native-languages.org/legends-turkey.htm.

18 Conrad, *Sapiens.org*.

19 Judith Shaw, "Turkey—Abundance, Gratitude and Connection to Mother Earth," *Feminism and Religion,* November 25, 2020, https:/ /feminismandreligion.com/2020/11/25/turkey-abundance-gratitude -and-connection-to-mother-earth-by-judith-shaw/.

20 Steven Foster and James A. Duke, *Eastern/Central Medicinal Plants and Herbs,* 2nd ed., Peterson Field Guides Series (New York: Houghton Mifflin. 2000), 209.

21 Juliet Blankespoor, *The Healing Garden: Cultivating & Handcrafting Herbal Remedies* (New York: Mariner Books, 2022), 226.

22 Foster and Duke, *Eastern/Central Medicinal Plants and Herbs,* 209

23 Blankespoor, *The Healing Garden,* 227.

24 James A. Duke, *The Green Pharmacy* (Emmaus, PA: Rodale Press, 1997), 78, 431.

25 Blankespoor, *The Healing Garden,* 223.

26 Blankespoor, *The Healing Garden,* 227.

August

1 "Lammas Day," *Almanac,* accessed December 5, 2023, https:/ /www.almanac.com/fact/lammas-day-from-the-old-english-holiday.

2 Amy Willis, "Today is Lammas in the UK—but do YOU know what that is?" *Metro,* December 12, 2019, https://metro.co.uk/2017/08/01/today- is-lammas-in-the-uk-but-do-you-know-what-that-is-6819690/.

3 "The Festival Sabbat of Lammas, Lughnassadh," *The Goddess and the Green Man,* July 26, 2022, https://www.goddessandgreenman.co.uk/blog/lammas.

4 Barbara Walker, *The Woman's Dictionary of Symbols and Sacred Objects* (San Francisco, CA: Harper Collins, 1988), 486.

5 Walker, *The Woman's Dictionary,* 198.

6 Patti Wigington, "Lammas History: Welcoming the Harvest," *Learn Religions,* April 29, 2019, https://www.learnreligions.com/history-of -the-lammas-harvest-celebration-2562170.

7 Walker, *The Woman's Dictionary,* 486.

8 Gail Faith Edwards, "Assumption Day—First Fruits Festival, Way of the Wild Heart," August 13, 2011, https://gailfaithedwards.com/2011/08/13 /assumption-day-first-fruits-festival/.

9 Sarah Kuta, "1,300-Year-Old Corn God Statue Shows How the Maya Worshipped Maize," *Smithsonian,* June 7, 2022, https://www .smithsonianmag.com/smart-news/1300-year-old-corn-god-statue -shows-how-maya-worshipped-maize-180980206/?utm_source =smithsoniandaily&utm_medium=email&utm_campaign=20220607 -daily-responsive&sp MailingID=46942298&spUserID=MTEoNTc2Njgx MjkoOQS2&spJobID=2260720122&spReportId=MjI2MDcyMDEyMgS2.

10 James Frazer, "The Golden Bough," *Wikisource* [Chapter 46, 413], accessed December 7, 2023, https://en.wikisource.org/wiki/ The_Golden_Bough/Corn-Mother_in_Many_Lands.

11 "Native American Maize (Corn) Mythology," *Native Languages of the Americas*, accessed December 7, 2023, http://www.native-languages.org /legends-corn.htm.

12 Tamra Andrews, *A Dictionary of Nature Myths* (New York: Oxford Press, 1998), 174–175.

13 "Dewi Sri, Nang Khosop and the Bountiful Body of a Goddess," *Martini Fisher*, August 21, 2020, https://martinifisher.com/2020/08/21/dewi -sri-and-nang-khosop-the-goddesses-who-gave-their-life-and-bodies -so-that-mankind-could-live/.

14 Kent Davis, "Rice Goddesses of Indonesia, Cambodia and Thailand," *Devata*, October 26, 2011, http://www.devata.org/rice-goddesses-of -indonesia-cambodia-and-thailand/ #.ZFFIMs7MLBU.

15 Miriam Robbins Dexter, "The Monstrous Goddess: The Degeneration of Ancient Bird and Snake Goddesses," *The Journal of Archaeomythology* 7 (Special Issue 2011): 181–202, https://www.archaeomythology.org/wp -content/uploads/2012/11/Dexter-7.pdf.

16 Juliet Blankespoor, *The Healing Garden: Cultivating & Handcrafting Herbal Remedies* (New York: Mariner Books, 2022), 271.

17 Rosalee de la Forêt and Emily Han, *Wild Remedies: How to Forage Healing Foods and Craft our Your Own Herbal Medicine* (New York: Hay House, 2020), 248.

18 James A. Duke, *The Green Pharmacy* (Emmaus, PA: Rodale Press, 1997), 198.

19 Duke, *The Green Pharmacy*, 136, 137, 146.

20 Duke, *The Green Pharmacy*, 425.

21 Kat Maier, *Energetic Herbalism: A Guide to Sacred Plant Traditions Integrating Elements of Vitalism, Ayurveda, and Chinese Medicine* (White River Junction, VT: Chelsea Green Publishing, 2021), 42, 141.

22 Maier, *Energetic Herbalism*, 144.

23 Maier, *Energetic Herbalism*, 98.

24 De la Forêt and Han, *Wild Remedies*, 245.

25 De la Forêt and Han, *Wild Remedies*, 248.

26 Blankespoor, *The Healing Garden*, 274.

27 Charles Eisenstein, *Sacred Economics: Money, Gift, and Society in the Age of Transition* (Berkeley, CA: Evolver Editions, 2011).

28 "What is Burning Man: The 10 Principles of Burning Man," *Burning Man Project*, accessed December 9, 2023, https://burningman.org /about/10-principles/.

September

1 Jack Kornfield, "The Sacred Pause," March 8, 2021, https://jackkornfield .com/the-sacred-pause/.

2 Parker J. Palmer, "There Is a Season: A Meditation on the Cycles of Our Inner Lives," *Fetzer Institute Retreat Center*, 9, https://fetzer.org/sites/default/files/2020–12/There%20Is%20a%20Season%20by%20Parker%20Palmer_web_0.pdf.

3 Palmer, "There Is a Season," 10.

4 Palmer, "There Is a Season," 11.

5 Kat Maier, *Energetic Herbalism: A Guide to Sacred Plant Traditions Integrating Elements of Vitalism, Ayurveda, and Chinese Medicine* (White River Junction, VT: Chelsea Green Publishing, 2021), 94–96.

6 "Mabon/Autumn Equinox September 21–22," *The Goddess and the Green Man*, July 30, 2022, https://www.goddessandgreenman.co.uk/blog/mabon-autumn-equinox-september-21–22.

7 Barbara Walker, *The Woman's Dictionary of Symbols and Sacred Objects* (San Francisco: HarperCollins, 1988), 90.

8 "Oktoberfest: German Festival," *Britannica*, accessed November 25, 2023, https://www.britannica.com/topic/Oktoberfest.

9 Jessi Roti, "Top 20 U.S. Cities to Visit for Oktoberfest," *Chicago Tribune*, September 15, 2016, https://www.chicagotribune.com/travel/chi-top-20-cities-for-oktoberfest-travel-0915-story.html.

10 Matt Stefon, "5 Harvest Festivals Around the World," *Britannica*, accessed December 9, 2023, https://www.britannica.com/list/5-harvest-festivals-around-the-world.

11 Victoria Philpott,"13 Best Festivals in September Around the World in 2024," *Vicky Flip Flop*, October 17, 2023, https://vickyflipfloptravels.com/festivals-in-september/.

12 Mayowa Oyewale, "West African Yam Festivals Celebrate Harvest, Community and Life Itself," *Modern Farmer*, April 18, 2023, https://modernfarmer.com/2023/04/west-african-yam-festivals/.

13 "Sukkot," Wikipedia, accessed December 9, 2023, https://en.wikipedia.org/wiki/Sukkot.

14 Erika Buenaflor, *Cleansing Rites of Curanderismo: Limpias Espirituales of Ancient Mesoamerican Shamans* (Rochester, VT: Bear & Company, 2018).

15 "Smudging Ceremony," *Powwow Power* (accessed December 9, 2023), https://powwow-power.com/smudging/.

16 John P. Rafferty, "9 of the World's Deadliest Spiders," *Britannica*, accessed December 9, 2023), https://www.britannica.com/list/9-of-the-worlds-deadliest-spiders.

17 Graham C. L. Davey, "Why Are We Afraid of Spiders?" *Psychology Today*, July 21, 2014, https://www.psychologytoday.com/gb/blog/why-we-worry/201407/why-are-we-afraid-spiders.

18 Tamra Andrews, *A Dictionary of Nature Myths* (New York: Oxford Press, 1998), 7.

19 Judika Illes, *The Encyclopedia of Spirits: The Ultimate Guide to the Magic of Fairies, Genies, Demons, Ghosts, Gods & Goddesses* (New York: Harper One, 2019), 176.

20 Linda Star Wolf and Anna Cariad-Barrett, *Sacred Medicine of Bee, Butterfly, Earthworm, and Spider: Shamanic Teachers of the Instar Medicine Wheel* (Rochester, VT: Bear & Co, 2013), 123–124.

21 Walker, *The Women's Dictionary*, 419–420.

22 "Nazca Lines," *Britannica*, accessed December 10, 2023, https://www.britannica.com/place/Nazca-Lines

23 Juliet Blankespoor, *The Healing Garden: Cultivating & Handcrafting Herbal Remedies* (New York: Mariner Books, 2022), 284.

24 Blankespoor, *The Healing Garden*, 284.

25 Maier, *Energetic Herbalism*, 254.

26 James A. Duke, *The Green Pharmacy* (Emmaus, PA: Rodale Press, 1997), 83–84, 208.

27 Maier, *Energetic Herbalism*, 256.

28 Maier, *Energetic Herbalism*, 257.

29 Blankespoor, *The Healing Garden*, 282.

30 "Climate Change 2021: The Physical Science Basis," *The Intergovernmental Panel on Climate Change (IPCC)*, accessed December 10, 2023, https://www.ipcc.ch/report/ar6/wg1/.

31 David Korten, "When Less Is More," *Yes Magazine*, August 12, 2021, https://www.yesmagazine.org/opinion/2021/08/12/consumption-climate-change-earth.

32 David Korten, "Ecological Civilization: From Emergency to Emergence," *Yes Magazine*, May 25, 2021, updated June 2022, https://www.yesmagazine.org/wp-content/uploads/2021/08/EcoCivFromE2EJune2021.pdf.

33 Paul Hawken, *Regeneration: Ending the Climate Crisis in One Generation* (New York: Penguin, 2021).

October

1 "Samhain/Halloween October 31," *The Goddess and The Green Man*, July 30, 2022, https://www.goddessandgreenman.co.uk/blog/samhain-halloween-october-31.

2 "Samhain/Halloween October 31," *The Goddess and The Green Man*.

3 Christine Valters Paintner, *Abbey of the Arts* newsletter, October 29, 2023, https://mailchi.mp/abbeyofthearts/listening-at-the-threshold-oct29-2023 quotes from her book: *The Love of Thousands: How Angels, Saints, and Ancestors Walk with Us Toward Holiness* (South Bend, IN: Ave Maria Press, 2023).

4 Logan Ward, "Top 10 Things to Know About the Day of the Dead," October 14, 2022, *National Geographic*, https://www.nationalgeographic.com/travel/article/top-ten-day-of-dead-mexico.

5 "Gray Squirrel," *Virginia Department of Wildlife Resources*, accessed August 18, 2023, https://dwr.virginia.gov/wildlife/information/gray-squirrel/.

6 "Red Squirrel," *Virginia Department of Wildlife Resources*, accessed August 18, 2023, https://dwr.virginia.gov/wildlife/information/red-squirrel/.

7   "Fox Squirrel," *Virginia Department of Wildlife Resources*, accessed August 18, 2023, https://dwr.virginia.gov/wildlife/information/fox-squirrel/.

8   "Virginia Northern Flying Squirrel," *Virginia Department of Wildlife Resources*, accessed January 4, 2024, https://dwr.virginia.gov/wildlife/information/virginia-northern-flying-squirrel/.

9   Sue Lindsey, "Benefits of wind power weighed against costs," *Herald-Tribune*, August 21, 2006, https://www.heraldtribune.com/story/news/2006/08/21/benefits-of-wind-power-weighed-against-costs/28496011007/.

10 "Southern Flying Squirrel," *Virginia Department of Wildlife Resources*, accessed January 4, 2024, https://dwr.virginia.gov/wildlife/information/southern-flying-squirrel/.

11 Christine Ennulat, "Secret Squirrel," *Virginia Living*, October 29, 2009, https://www.virginialiving.com/culture/secret-squirrel/.

12 Lori Lovely, "How to Keep Squirrels Out of Garden Beds and Potted Plants," November 14, 2023, *BobVila*, https://www.bobvila.com/articles/how-to-keep-squirrels-out-of-garden/.

13 "Squirrels," *Virginia Places*, accessed January 6, 2024, http://www.virginiaplaces.org/natural/squirrels.html.

14 "Squirrels," *Virginia Places*.

15 Jamie Sams and David Carson, *Medicine Cards*, rev. ed. (New York: St. Martin's, 1999), 141.

16 Juliet Blankespoor, "Spiced Hawthorn Pear Persimmon Brandy," *Chestnut School of Herbal Medicine*, November 15, 2023, https://chestnutherbs.com/spiced-hawthorn-pear-persimmon-brandy/.

17 Steven Horne, "Hawthorn: Heart Health and Beyond," *Steven Horne Creations*, February 2, 2021, https://stevenhorne.com/article/Hawthorn-Heart-Health-and-Beyond.

18 Blankespoor, "Spiced Hawthorn Pear Persimmon Brandy."

19 Blankespoor, "Spiced Hawthorn Pear Persimmon Brandy."

20 Corinna Wood, "Hawthorne Berry as Herbal Medicine for Healing Your Heart," *Wise Woman Studies with Corinna Wood*, accessed January 9, 2024, https://www.corinnawood.com/blog/hawthorne-berry.

21 Blankespoor, "Spiced Hawthorn Pear Persimmon Brandy."

22 Blankespoor, "Spiced Hawthorn Pear Persimmon Brandy."

23 Horne, "Hawthorn: Heart Health and Beyond."

24 Duke, *The Green Pharmacy* (Emmaus, PA: Rodale, 1997), 44.

25 Duke, *The Green Pharmacy*, 45.

26 Duke, *The Green Pharmacy*, 246.

27 Duke, *The Green Pharmacy*, 300.

28 Horne, "Hawthorn: Heart Health and Beyond."

29 Horne, "Hawthorn: Heart Health and Beyond."

30 Kat Maier, *Energetic Herbalism: A Guide to Sacred Plant Traditions Integrating Elements of Vitalism, Ayurveda, and Chinese Medicine* (White River Junction, VT: Chelsea Green Publishing, 2021), 265.

31 Horne, "Hawthorn: Heart Health and Beyond."

32 Blankespoor, "Spiced Hawthorn Pear Persimmon Brandy."

33 Maier, *Energetic Herbalism*, 265.

34 Scott R. Loss, Tom Will, and Peter P. Marra, "The impact of free-ranging domestic cats on wildlife of the United States," *Nature Communications* 4, no. 1396 (January 29, 2013), DOI: 10.1038/ncomms2380, https:/ /dariuszzdziebk.wpenginepowered.com/wp-content/uploads/2015/09 /Loss_et_al._2013-Impacts_Outdoor_Cats.pdf.

November

1 Michael R. Hamblin, Cleber Ferraresi, Huang Ying-Ying, Lucas Freitas de Freitas, and James D. Carroll, *Low-Level Light Therapy: Photobiomodulation* (Bellingham, WA: International Society for Optics and Photonics, 2018), 16.

2 Ari Whitten, *The Ultimate Guide To Red Light Therapy: How to Use Red and Near-Infrared Light Therapy for Anti-Aging, Fat Loss, Muscle Gain, Performance Enhancement, and Brain Optimization* (Scotts Valley, CA: CreateSpace, 2018), 4.

3 Niina Niskanen, "Divine Grandmothers in Myths and Folklore," *Patheos*, October 16, 2022, https://www.patheos.com/blogs /mythsandfolklore/2022/01/divine-grandmothers-in-myths-and-folklore/.

4 Judika Illes, *The Encyclopedia of Spirits: The Ultimate Guide to the Magic of Fairies, Genies, Demons, Ghosts, Gods & Goddesses* (New York: Harper One, 2019), 806–807.

5 Barbara G. Walker, *The Crone: Woman of Age, Wisdom, and Power* (New York: HarperCollins, 1985), 21.

6 Walker, *The Crone*, 14.

7 Walker, *The Crone*, 38.

8 Walker, *The Crone*, 22.

9 Walker, *The Crone*, 30.

10 Clarissa Pinkola Estés, *Women Who Run With the Wolves: Myths and Stories of the Wild Woman Archetype* (New York: Ballantine, 1992), 93.

11 Estés, *Women Who Run With the Wolves*, 97–98.

12 Roger Tory Peterson, *Peterson Field Guide: Eastern Birds*, 4th ed. (Boston/New York: Houghton Mifflin Co, 1980), 206.

13 Ted Andrews, *Animal-Speak: The Spiritual & Magical Powers of Creatures Great & Small* (St. Paul, MN: Llewellyn Publications, 1998), 130–131, 188.

14 Andrews, *Animal-Speak*, 188.

15 "Kutkh" *Wikipedia*, accessed January 15, 2024, https://en.wikipedia.org /wiki/Kutkh.

16 Illes, *The Encyclopedia of Spirits*, 779.

17 Andrews, *Animal-Speak*, 187.

18 Anny Papatheodorou, "The Wisdom and Knowledge of the Shrewd Raven: Symbolism and Insights from Mythology," *Triple Moon Psychotherapy*, accessed January 15, 2024, https://www.triplemoonpsychotherapy.com/archetypes-and-symbolism-myth-and-psyche/raven-symbolism-dreamwork-and-meanings.

19 Andrews, *Animal-Speak*, 130.

20 Estés, *Women Who Run With the Wolves*, 101.

21 Michael Castleman, *The New Healing Herbs* (Emmaus, PA: Rodale, 2001), 414.

22 Castleman, *The New Healing Herbs*, 414.

23 Mary Plantwalker, "The Folklore and Medicine of Witch Hazel," *Chestnut School of Herbal Medicine*, November 24, 2023, https://chestnutherbs.com/the-folklore-and-medicine-of-witch-hazel/.

24 Castleman, *The New Healing Herbs*, 414.

25 Plantwalker, "The Folklore and Medicine of Witch Hazel."

26 James Duke, *The Green Pharmacy* (Emmaus, PA: Rodale Press, 1997), 100, 251, 395, 417, 447, 459.

27 Sam Coffman, *The Herbal Medic: Practical, Clinical Herbalism & First Aid: For Home, Remote and Post-disaster Environments*, Volume 1 (San Antonio, TX: The Human Path, 2014), 173.

28 Foster, Steven, *Witch Hazel Monograph* (accessed January 15, 2024), https://www.stevenfoster.com/education/monograph/witchhazel.html.

29 Claire Murshima, "People here live in complete darkness for 2.5 months. Here's how they do it," *Morning Edition*, November 13, 2022, https://www.npr.org/2022/11/11/1135994636/polar-night-winter-darkness-tips?utm_source=npr_newsletter&utm_medium=email&utm_content=20221120&utm_term=7558816&utm_campaign=best-of-npr&utm_id=31908778&orgid=1307&utm_att1=.

30 "Northerners cope in different ways with prolonged winter darkness," *Eye on the Arctic, Yle News*, updated December 7, 2018, https://www.rcinet.ca/eye-on-the-arctic/2018/12/04/finland-north-winter-darkness-health-depression-sunlight-coping/.

31 Murshima, "People here live in complete darkness."

32 Linda Åkeson McGurk, *The Open-Air Life: Discover the Nordic Art of Friluftsliv and Embrace Nature Every Day* (New York: Random House, 2022).

33 "Polar Bear Plunge Day—January 1, 2024," *National Today*, accessed January 18, 2024, https://nationaltoday.com/polar-bear-plunge-day/.

December

1 Ingrid Fetell Lee, *Joyful: The Surprising Power of Ordinary Things to Create Extraordinary Happiness* (New York: Little, Brown Spark, 2018), 19.

2 Marcie Telander, "When Santa was a Woman and Rebirth of the Sun—Spirits of the Winter Solstice 2011," accessed January 20, 2024, http://www.marcietelander.com/earth-celebrations.html.

3 Beth Daley, "What Winter Solstice Rituals Tell us about Indigenous People," *The Conversation*, December 13, 2018, https://theconversation.com/what-winter-solstice-rituals-tell-us-about-indigenous-people-108327?fbclid=IwAR0MiANJBxKwhSEDN0X6W-mdrIbF-dU93GVGAmTiNuLAPE9X4UgXfAsngDw.

4 Charles Fréger, *Wilder Mann: the Image of the Savage* (Stockport, UK: Dewi Lewis Publishing, 2012).

5 "Krampus," *Wikipedia*, accessed January 21, 2024, https://en.wikipedia.org/wiki/Krampus.

6 "Knecht Ruprecht," *Wikipedia*, accessed January 21, 2024, https://en.wikipedia.org/wiki/Knecht_Ruprecht.

7 "Zwarte Piet," *Wikipedia*, accessed January 21, 2024, https://en.wikipedia.org/wiki/Zwarte_Piet.

8 Anna Muckerman, "The Man Behind the Krampus Mask," *BBC*, December 8, 2018, https://www.bbc.com/travel/article/20181206-the-man-behind-the-krampus-mask.

9 "Krampus," *Wikipedia*.

10 Daley, "Winter Solstice Rituals."

11 Guy Underwood, *The Pattern of the Past* (London: Museum Press, 1969), quoted by Monica Sjöö and Barbara Mor, *The Great Cosmic Mother: Rediscovering the Religion of the Earth* (San Francisco: HarperCollins, 1991), 124.

12 Sjöö and Mor, *The Great Cosmic Mother*, 125–126.

13 Esther Jacobson, *The Deer Goddess of Ancient Siberia: A Study in the Ecology of Belief* (Leiden, The Netherlands: E.J.Brill), 1993.

14 Telander, "When Santa was a Woman."

15 Danielle P. Olson, "Doe, a Deer, a Female Reindeer: The Spirit of Winter Solstice," *Gather Victoria*, December 12, 2017, https://gathervictoria.com/2017/12/15/doe-a-deer-a-female-deer-the-spirit-of-mother-christmas/?fbclid=IwAR3uGaT8FH4ByscAhr5m5SqSFf_Dxz0EPfe7KMDUgtGTJJyChQrQJeOlAMc.

16 "Siberian Princess Reveals Her 2,500 Year Old Tattoos," *The Siberian Times*, August 14, 2012, https://siberiantimes.com/culture/others/features/siberian-princess-reveals-her-2500-year-old-tattoos/.

17 Olson, "Doe, a Deer, a Female Reindeer."

18 Judika Illes, *The Encyclopedia of Spirits: The Ultimate Guide to the Magic of Fairies, Genies, Demons, Ghosts, Gods & Goddesses* (New York: Harper One, 2019), 885.

19 Olson, "Doe, a Deer."

20 "Reindeer People," *Slice* (Documentary), Hamid Sardar, director, August 15, 2021, https://www.youtube.com/watch?v=Tv144ggxRGA.

21 Nila Sweeney, "The Dukha: Last of Mongolia's reindeer people," *CNN*, September 29, 2016, https://www.cnn.com/travel/article/dukha-last-reindeer-people/index.html.

22 Tanya Dewey, "Odocoileus virginianus: White-Tailed Deer," *Animal Diversity Web*, accessed January 25, 2024, https://animaldiversity.org/accounts/Odocoileus_virginianus/html.

23 Dewey, "White-Tailed Deer."

24 "White-tailed Deer: Odocoileus virginianus," *Chesapeake Bay Program*, accessed January 31, 2024, https://www.chesapeakebay.net/discover/field-guide/entry/white-tailed-deer.

25 "White-tailed Deer," *Chesapeake Bay Program*.

26 "Pinus Genus (Pine)," Conifer Database, *American Conifer Society*, accessed January 31, 2024, https://conifersociety.org/conifers/pinus/.

27 Steve Nix, "Identifying Common North American Conifers," *Treehugger*, June 14, 2022, https://www.treehugger.com/id-most-common-north-american-conifers-1341840.

28 Juliet Blankespoor, "The Medicine of Pine," *Chestnut School of Herbal Medicine*, November 23, 2023, https://chestnutherbs.com/themedicine-of-pine/.

29 Rosalee de la Forêt, *Herbs with Rosalee* (Rosalee de la Forêt, LLC, Methow Valley, WA, first digital edition, December 2021), https://delaforet.s3.us-west-2.amazonaws.com/ebook-YT-Pine-Needle-Tea-merged.pdf.

30 Blankespoor, "The Medicine of Pine."

31 "Pinus Genus (Pine)," American Conifer Society.

32 Blankespoor, "The Medicine of Pine."

33 De la Forêt, *Herbs with Rosalee*.

34 Blankespoor, "The Medicine of Pine."

35 "Pine Herbal Monograph," *Natural Herbal Living*, August 11, 2022, https://naturalherballiving.com/pine-herbal-monograph/?fbclid=IwAR199gXDbTOx7SioSwk-u7tgDHoeyrxtJbw_clAPc3fw3k-BSzUPhJwTn4c.

36 De la Forêt, *Herbs with Rosalee*.

37 Blankespoor, "The Medicine of Pine."

38 "Raunacht," *Wikipedia*, accessed Feb 2, 2024, https://de.wikipedia.org/wiki/Raunacht.

39 "Wilde Jagd," *Wikipedia*, accessed February 2, 2024, https://de.wikipedia.org/wiki/Wilde_Jagd.

40 "Rauhnächte - In Germany, it's the Time Between the Years," *German Girl in America*, accessed Feb 2, 2024, https://germangirlinamerica.com/what-is-rauhnacht/.

41 "Bleigießen," *Wikipedia*, accessed Feb 2, 2024, https://de.wikipedia.org/wiki/Bleigie%C3%9Fen.

SELECTED BIBLIOGRAPHY

This section summarizes books referred to in the text and others that expanded my thinking but were not cited. Blogs and similar online sources including personal communications are only included in the Endnotes.

Ackerman, Diane. *A Natural History of the Senses*. New York: Vintage, 1991.

Adler, Tamar. *An Everlasting Meal: Cooking with Economy and Grace*. New York: Scribner, 2011.

Andrews, Tamra. *A Dictionary of Nature Myths*. New York: Oxford University Press, 1998.

Andrews, Ted. *Animal-Speak: The Spiritual & Magical Powers of Creatures Great & Small*. St. Paul, MN: Llewellyn Publications, 1998.

Blair, Nancy. *Amulets of the Goddess*. Oakland, CA: Wingbow, 1993.

Blankespoor, Juliet. *The Healing Garden: Cultivating & Handcrafting Herbal Remedies*. New York: Mariner Books, 2022.

Bonneau, Anne-Marie. *The Zero-Waste Chef: Plant-Forward Recipes and Tips for a Sustainable Kitchen and Planet*. New York: Avery, 2021.

Brody, Hugh. *The Other Side of Eden: Hunters, Farmers, and the Shaping of the World*. New York: North Point Press, 2000.

Buenaflor, Erika. *Cleansing Rites of Curanderismo: Limpias Espirituales of Ancient Mesoamerican Shamans*. Rochester, VT: Bear & Company, 2018.

Castleman, Michael. *The New Healing Herbs*. Emmaus, PA: Rodale, 2001.

Coffman, Sam. *The Herbal Medic: Practical, Clinical Herbalism & First Aid: For Home, Remote and Post-disaster Environments*, vol.1. San Antonio, TX: The Human Path, 2014.

Cohen, Michael J. *Reconnecting With Nature*. Lakeville, MN: Ecopress, 2007.

Coperthwaite, William. *A Handmade Life: In Search of Simplicity*. White River Junction, VT: Chelsea Green, 2007.

De la Forêt, Rosalee, and Emily Han. *Wild Remedies: How to Forage Healing Foods and Craft Your Own Herbal Medicine*. New York: Hay House, 2020.

Duke, James A., PhD. *The Green Pharmacy*. Emmaus, PA: Rodale, 1997.

Eisenstein, Charles. *Sacred Economics: Money, Gift, and Society in the Age of Transition*. Berkeley, CA: Evolver Editions, 2011.

Estés, Clarissa Pinkola. *Women Who Run With the Wolves: Myths and Stories of the Wild Woman Archetype*. New York: Ballantine, 1992.

Foster, Steven, and James A. Duke. *Eastern/Central Medicinal Plants and Herbs*, 2nd ed., Peterson Field Guides Series. New York: Houghton Mifflin, 2000.

Fréger, Charles. *Wilder Mann: The Image of the Savage*. Stockport, UK: Dewi Lewis Publishing, 2012.

Hamblin, Michael, R., Cleber Ferraresi, Huang Ying-Ying, Lucas Freitas de Freitas, and James D. Carroll. *Low-Level Light Therapy: Photobiomodulation*. Bellingham, WA: International Society for Optics and Photonics, 2018.

Hawken, Paul. *Regeneration: Ending the Climate Crisis in One Generation*. New York: Penguin, 2021.

Illes, Judika. *The Encyclopedia of Spirits: The Ultimate Guide to the Magic of Fairies, Genies, Demons, Ghosts, Gods & Goddesses*. New York: Harper One, 2019.

Jacobson, Esther. *The Deer Goddess of Ancient Siberia: A Study in the Ecology of Belief*. Leiden, The Netherlands: E.J. Brill, 1993.

Kallas, John. *Edible Wild Plants: Wild Foods from Dirt to Plate.* Layton, UT: Gibbs Smith, 2010.

Kraft, Jessica Carew. *Why We Need to Be Wild: One Woman's Quest for Ancient Human Answers to 21st Century Problems.* Naperville, IL: Sourcebooks, 2023.

Lee, Ingrid Fetell. *Joyful: The Surprising Power of Ordinary Things to Create Extraordinary Happiness.* New York: Little, Brown Spark, 2018.

Maier, Kat. *Energetic Herbalism: A Guide to Sacred Plant Traditions Integrating Elements of Vitalism, Ayurveda, and Chinese Medicine.* White River Junction, VT: Chelsea Green, 2021.

McGurk, Linda Åkeson. *The Open-Air Life: Discover the Nordic Art of Friluftsliv and Embrace Nature Every Day.* New York: Random House, 2022.

Montenegro, Nina, and Sonya Montenegro. *Mending Life: A Handbook for Repairing Clothes and Hearts.* Seattle: Sasquatch Books, 2020.

Neumann, E. *The Great Mother.* Princeton, NJ: Princeton University Press, 1974.

Owusu, Heike. *Symbols of Native America.* New York: Sterling, 1997.

Paintner, Christine Valters. *The Love of Thousands: How Angels, Saints, and Ancestors Walk with Us Toward Holiness.* South Bend, IN: Ave Maria, 2023.

Peterson, Roger Tory. *Peterson Field Guide: Eastern Birds*, 4th ed. Boston/New York: Houghton Mifflin, 1980.

Robinson, Jo. *Eating On the Wild Side: The Missing Link to Optimum Health.* New York: Little, Brown, 2013.

Sams, Jamie, and David Carson. *Medicine Cards.* New York: St. Martin's, 1999.

Scott, Timothy Lee. *Invasive Plant Medicine: The Ecological Benefits and Healing Abilities of Invasives.* Rochester, VT: Healing Arts, 2010.

Sjöö, Monica and Barbara Mor. *The Great Cosmic Mother: Rediscovering the Religion of the Earth.* San Francisco, CA: Harper/Collins, 1991.

Spelman, Elizabeth V. *Repair: The Impulse to Restore in a Fragile World.* Boston: Beacon, 2002.

Star Wolf, Linda, and Anna Cariad-Barrett. *Sacred Medicine of Bee, Butterfly, Earthworm, and Spider: Shamanic Teachers of the Instar Medicine Wheel.* Rochester, VT: Bear & Co, 2013.

Tallamy, Douglas W. *Bringing Nature Home: How You Can Sustain Wildlife with Native Plants.* Portland, OR: Timber Press, 2013.

Underwood, Guy. *The Pattern of the Past.* London: Museum Press, 1969.

Walker, Barbara G. *The Crone: Woman of Age, Wisdom, and Power.* New York: HarperCollins, 1985.

Walker, Barbara G. *The Woman's Dictionary of Symbols and Sacred Objects.* San Francisco, CA: Harper Collins, 1988.

Werness, Hope B. *The Continuum Encyclopedia of Animal Symbolism in Art.* New York: Continuum, 2004.

Whitten, Ari. *The Ultimate Guide to Red Light Therapy: How to Use Red and Near-Infrared Light Therapy for Anti-Aging, Fat Loss, Muscle Gain, Performance Enhancement, and Brain Optimization.* Scotts Valley, CA: CreateSpace, 2018.

Whyte, David. *Consolations: The Solace, Nourishment and Underlying Meaning of Everyday Words.* Langley, WA: Many Rivers, 2015.

Wilde, Mo. *The Wilderness Cure: Ancient Wisdom in a Modern World.* New York: Simon & Schuster, 2022.

Young, Jon. *What the Robin Knows: How Birds Reveal the Secrets of the Natural World.* Boston, MA: Houghton Mifflin Harcourt, 2012.

ACKNOWLEDGMENTS

This book has been a labor of love, and sometimes just plain hard labor, taking years to complete. I want to thank my husband, Dan, for his patience and unwavering support, not just with this book but also for our homesteading and rewilding adventures over the last twenty years. Deep appreciation to Asma for her steadfast friendship over the years and for sharing a beautiful place by the ocean for our annual writing retreats.

Long before I had any inkling that I would write a book, there were individuals who guided me: Frau Eva Liebich, my favorite elementary school teacher, who recognized my potential (yet still gave me a C in handwriting) and talked my parents into transferring me to higher-level education. Herr Eberhard Schmitz, my German teacher at the Richard Wagner Gymnasium in Baden-Baden, who challenged me to think critically and analytically. His Socratic method of teaching was often exasperating but effective in the long run. I also want to acknowledge my first college-level English teacher, Mrs. Nora Kueppers, who encouraged me when I was just beginning to write in English, my second language, and still confused a lot of prepositions. We continue to be in contact more than forty years after that first English 101 class at the University of Maryland, Heidelberg division. Frau Liebich, Herr Schmitz, and Mrs. Kueppers are examples of the deep and lasting impact outstanding teachers can have on their students, and I am so lucky that they were in my life at important crossroads.

Gratitude to my more recent writing teacher, Laura Davis, and the women in her online writers' feedback group who generously provided feedback on various portions of this book. Much appreciation to others who read the manuscript or portions of it and helped improve it: Rhet Wilson, Ralph Thönißen, Dan Kauffman, Kwanza Msingwana, Michael Watson, John Fox, Joyce Kornblatt,

Mo Wilde, and Thea Summer Deer. A very special thanks to LA Bourgeois, my book coach, who helped me stay organized and motivated and always surprised and delighted me with yet another creative idea out of her large coaching tool box.

Many thanks to my publishing team at Bold Story Press, especially my developmental editor, Nedah Rose, for bringing it all together, and Emily Barrosse for accepting my book for publication.

Much appreciation to my fellow nature writers who provided support, answered many questions, and shared mistakes so I wouldn't have to make them myself: Leah Rampy, Jessica Carew Kraft, Mary Reynolds Thompson, Georgann Eubanks, and Kat Maier.

Thank you to many others whose brains I picked about the publishing process and writing in general, especially in the early stages: Dawn Field, Cynthia Atkins, Erik Sax, Musa Murawih, Melissa Kaplan, and Nancy Sorrels.

I suspect that I may be leaving out some people. Just know that if you have been in my life, you left an imprint, and I am thankful for it. When I think of all the people I mentioned here who influenced my writing and thinking, I am in awe of the web of interconnection that exists not only between us humans but also between us and the more-than-human world. I am beyond grateful for the privilege of living on the land that calls us and teaches us so much.

ABOUT THE AUTHOR

Annette Naber, PhD, was born and raised in Germany and emigrated to the US to attend college and graduate school. After retiring from her successful psychology career in the Washington DC area, she and her husband moved to the Virginia Highlands, where she established organic gardens, an edible landscape, and a native plant sanctuary on their property. Here she immerses herself more deeply in nature therapies and incorporates symbolism, multisensory awareness, journaling, and crafts into her workshops and retreats. Naber is also a nature photographer who has exhibited her work in the Shenandoah Valley and the Virginia Highlands region. She has published mental health articles in local papers, nature reconnection techniques in *Psychology Today*, and photo essays on her blog www.Beauty AlongtheRoad.wordpress.com. *Seasons of a Wild Life* is her first book. Her author website is https://annettenaber.com/.

ABOUT BOLD STORY PRESS

Bold Story Press is a curated, woman-owned hybrid publishing company with a mission of publishing well-written stories by women. If your book is chosen for publication, our team of expert editors and designers will work with you to publish a professionally edited and designed book. Every woman has a story to tell. If you have written yours and want to explore publishing with Bold Story Press, contact us at https://boldstorypress.com.

BOLD STORY PRESS

The Bold Story Press logo, designed by Grace Arsenault, was inspired by the nom de plume, or pen name, a sad necessity at one time for female authors who wanted to publish. The woman's face hidden in the quill is the profile of Virginia Woolf, who, in addition to being an early feminist writer, founded and ran her own publishing company, Hogarth Press.

www.ingramcontent.com/pod-product-compliance
Lightning Source LLC
Chambersburg PA
CBHW072134270326
41931CB00010B/1758